About The Author

Nhyira Premium is an impeccable Business Educator, Author and Entrepreneur by Purpose. He is a Self-Motivated and Self-Educated individual with many years of expert experience in Accountancy and Finance both in the Education industry (as a Lecturer) and in the Corporate World.

He is the Chief Executive Officer of Premium Education Hub, an Education and Business consultancy firm serving clients and students across the globe using Technology and Information Systems. His passion as an Educator is to help students across the globe excel academically in Examination and also become the best in the Corporate World. It is this passion that has led him to write pragmatic Business Books for students at different levels on the Education ladder.

Nhyira is a Manager of some Start-up Companies and a member on the Board of Trustees of some Non-Governmental Organisations (NGOs) in Ghana.

He is also a Philanthropist who belief the only way to eradicate poverty in Ghana and Africa is to provide Human Capacity Building and Entrepreneurial Skills to individuals in the Society and set them up to become well equipped to manage their own affairs. This is why he organizes Conferences, Mentorship and Coaching sessions for individuals to empower them to become self – sustained people in their respective Communities. This in the long term will result into Economic growth, creation of jobs and increase the revenue of Government through taxation to provide State of the Art Infrastructure facilities and Social amenities, thereby bridging the gap between the rich and the poor; the literate and illiterate.

Nhyira is a Christian, fellowships with the International Central Gospel Church (Christ Temple) and sits under the Leadership and Ministry of Dr. Mensa Otabil.

TEL: +233(0)548769918 /+233 (0) 501149296
Facebook Page: www.facebook.com/premiumicaglobal
Website: www.premiumonlinehub.com

He is also a Minister of the Gospel and a Motivational Speaker, travels around preaching and speaking in conferences.

Nhyira lives in Accra, Ghana with his family.

Other Books by the Author

- ➢ *Strategic Management*
- ➢ *Public Sector Accounting and Finance*
- ➢ *Financial Management*
- ➢ *Advanced Audit and Assurance*
- ➢ *Management Accounting*
- ➢ *Corporate Reporting*
- ➢ *Financial Reporting*
- ➢ *Advance Financial Management*
- ➢ *Quantitative Tools in Business*

For more information:

Call: +233 (0) 548769918 / +233 (0) 501149296

Visit: www.premiumonlinehub.com

Facebook: www.facebook.com/premiumicaglobal

PEC, walking the journey with you!!!!!!!

TEL: +233(0)548769918 /+233 (0) 501149296
Facebook Page: www.facebook.com/premiumicaglobal
Website: www.premiumonlinehub.com

Preface

It has come to the notice of the general public and especially the students of the Institute of Chartered Accountants – Ghana (ICA –GH) about the unavailability of a precise and concise study manual specifically for the Institute's subject 'PUBLIC SECTOR ACCOUNTING AND FINANCE'.

Although the institute has recommended some books to students to buy and study to enable them prepare for the exams, these books contain a lot of 'non-syllabus' items which makes studying the subject quite cumbersome. Students continue to complain because, they prepare and study a lot of things but enter the exams hall with very little to write for the allotted marks for a question. This has caused a lot of students failing the exams over the years.

This 'menace' has come to the notice of Premium Education and Business Consult (PEC), an online Education and Business Consultancy firm and so we decided to begin a journey of addressing the problem by writing a single study text which is purely relevant to the ICA-GH examination.

In an attempt to address the problem, we decided to produce this study text which is still a work-in-progress to enable all candidates focus on key areas of the syllabus and gain specific knowledge as required by the Institute. We are by no means regarding the study texts recommended by the Institute as not appropriate for the preparation of the examination but we belief that our study text contains only what is required by each student preparing for the Public Sector Accounting and Finance examination.

With this study text in your hand, you can be guaranteed of a precise knowledge and higher possibilities of passing your examination and going to the next level.

THE AUTHOR

TEL: +233(0)548769918 /+233 (0) 501149296
Facebook Page: www.facebook.com/premiumicaglobal
Website: www.premiumonlinehub.com

Acknowledgement

The team at Premium Education Hub is grateful to the Almighty God for bestowing upon it this responsibility.

We also want to thank all our students who continue to request quality and standard materials from the organisation. To you all we, God bless you indeed!!!

We also want to thank Mr. Eric Folly for the contributions and recommendations made during the writing of this book. We say God bless you!!

We want to thank all other people who helped this project to become a reality. Because, without your sacrifices, contribution and recommendations, this project would have remained in the 'INCUBATOR' of the organisation.

We dedicate this project to all the staff and students on Premium Education and Business Consult.

TEL: +233(0)548769918 /+233 (0) 501149296
Facebook Page: www.facebook.com/premiumicaglobal
Website: www.premiumonlinehub.com

TABLE OF CONTENT

TEL: +233(0)548769918 /+233 (0) 501149296
Facebook Page: www.facebook.com/premiumicaglobal
Website: www.premiumonlinehub.com

INTRODUCTION TO PUBLIC SECTOR ACCOUNTING AND FINANCE

1.1. DEFINITION OF TERMS

Public Sector Accounting (ACC 310), introduced the simplest definition of 'Public Sector' is "all organisations which are not privately owned and operated, but which are established, run and financed by Government on behalf of the public."

R A Adams (2004) in his book "Public Sector Accounting and Finance Made Simple" defines Public Sector Accounting as "a process of recording, communicating, summarizing, analysing and interpreting Government financial statements and statistics in aggregate and details; it is concerned with the receipts, custody and disbursement and rendering of stewardship on public funds entrusted".

Government refers to the collection of public institutions established and given the authority to run the affairs of a country. It is a system of governance and includes the body of individuals who are authorised to administer the laws of a Nation.

Government Accounting refers to all the financial documents and records of public institutions that relate to the collection of tax payers" money, and the analysis, control of expenditure, administration of trust funds, management of government stores and all the financial responsibilities and duties of the relevant organs.

Government accounting includes the process of recording, analysing, classifying, summarising, communicating and interpreting financial information about Government in aggregate and in details, recording all transactions involving the receipt, transfer and disposition of public funds and property. The processes of Government Accounting are further discussed as follows:

TEL: +233(0)548769918 /+233 (0) 501149296
Facebook Page: www.facebook.com/premiumicaglobal
Website: www.premiumonlinehub.com

(a) **Recording**: Recording involves the process of documenting the financial transactions and activities in the necessary books of accounts are cash book, ledger and vote book.

(b) **Analysing**: Analysing involves the process of separating transactions according to their distinct nature and posting them under appropriate heads and sub-heads.

(c) **Classifying** : Classifying has to do with the grouping of the transactions into revenue and expense descriptions and bringing them under major classes as 'Revenue Head' and 'Sub-heads', with their relevant code numbers of accounts.

(d) **Summarising:** Summarising concerns the bringing together of all the classes of accounts and preparing them into reports periodically as are statutorily or organisationally required.

(e) **Communicating**: Communicating is about making available financial reports on all the government financial activities from the necessary accounting summaries to various interested parties. The style of communication adopted should be un-ambiguous, lucid and devoid of jargons as much as possible.

(f) **Interpreting**: Interpreting ends the process by giving explanations on what has been reported in the various financial statements and reports, as regards the overall operations and performance of the relevant government organisation(s). This is to enable the necessary parties and users to take relevant decisions based on their assessments of the reports.

TEL: +233(0)548769918 /+233 (0) 501149296
Facebook Page: www.facebook.com/premiumicaglobal
Website: www.premiumonlinehub.com

1.2. Public Sector Organisations exist for the following reasons:

(i) To provide public goods and services to individuals and institutional consumers regardless of their ability to pay

(ii) To provide good and services whose investment capital is quite high and hence cannot be provided by the private sector or whose returns are low and therefore unattractive to the private sector, though necessary

(iii) To achieve a net social benefit rather than net profit so as to enhance equity of access to meeting needs of water, electricity, food, shelter, transport, health and communication, etc.

(iv) To correct inequalities which exist among various social classes and communities

(v) To influence future social, political, economic or financial environment for optimal growth of the economy.

1.3. Types of Public Sector Organizations

Public sector organizations may exist at any of four levels:

- International (multistate entities or partnerships)
- National (an independent state)
- Regional (a province/state within a national state)
- Local (a municipal-level body such as a metropolis, municipality or district)

TEL: +233(0)548769918 /+233 (0) 501149296
Facebook Page: www.facebook.com/premiumicaglobal
Website: www.premiumonlinehub.com

At any of these levels, the public sector generally consists of at least three types of organizations:

a. **Central government** consists of a governing body with a defined territorial authority.

Central government includes all departments, ministries, and agencies of the government that are integral parts of the structure, and are accountable to and report directly to the central authority — the legislature, council, cabinet, or executive head.

b. **Boards, Authorities, & Commissions** consist of public organizations that are clearly part of the government and deliver public programs, goods, or services, but that exist as separate organizations in their own right — possibly as legal entities — and operate with a partial degree of operational independence. They often, but not necessarily, are headed by a board of directors, commission, or other appointed body. Examples are Electoral commission, Mineral commission, Ghana Atomic Agency Commission, etc.

c. **Local government:** This is made up of the local authorities such as Metropolitan assemblies, Municipal Assemblies and District Assemblies.

1.4. WAYS BY WHICH GOVERNMENT CONTROL PUBLIC COMPANIES

i.   Government powers can be exercised through the appointment of Chief Executives and members of Boards of management

ii.   Government can exercise control by giving specific directions concerning prices production costs and social goals.

iii. Government uses the submission of annual reports as an opportunity to evaluate the performance of enterprises

iv.   Public companies need to obtain government approvals and guarantees for long term loans

TEL: +233(0)548769918 /+233 (0) 501149296
Facebook Page: www.facebook.com/premiumicaglobal
Website: www.premiumonlinehub.com

v.   Public companies need to obtain government approval for their annual budgets.

vi.   Government may specify the economic roles of state enterprises and the target rates of their return.

1.5. NATURE AND OBJECTIVES OF GOVERNMENT ACCOUNTING

The objectives of Government accounting include the following:

(a) **To fulfil legal requirement**: The law requires that government accounts are prepared and audited annually.

(b) **To perform the stewardship function**: The ruling government is the steward of the resources and finances of the Nation. Government has to give account of how these finances are used.

(c) To enable Government to plan well the future activities and programmes of the Nation.

(d) To provide a process of controlling the use of the financial and other resources.

(e) To provide the means by which actual performance may be compared with the target set.

(f) To evaluate the economy, efficiency and effectiveness with which governance is carried out.

1.6. PURPOSE OF PUBLIC SECTOR ACCOUNTING

The purposes of Public Sector Accounting include:

1. Demonstrating the proprietary of transactions and their conformity with the law, established rules and regulations.

2. Measuring current performance.

3. Providing useful information for the efficient control and effective management of government operations.

TEL: +233(0)548769918 /+233 (0) 501149296
Facebook Page: www.facebook.com/premiumicaglobal
Website: www.premiumonlinehub.com

4. Facilitating audit exercise to be carried out.

5. Planning future operations.

6. Appraising those in the authority, in efficiency and effectiveness

1.7. OBJECTIVES OF PUBLIC SECTOR ACCOUNTING

The main purposes of Public Sector Accounting are:

(a) Ascertaining the legitimacy of transactions and their compliance with the established norms, regulations and statutes.
(b) Providing evidence of stewardship.
(c) Assisting planning and control.
(d) Assisting objective and timely reporting.
(e) Providing the basis for decision-making.
(f) Enhancing the appraisal of the efficiency of management.
(g) Highlighting the various sources of revenue receivable and the expenditure to be incurred.
(h) Identifying the sources of funding capital projects.
(i) Evaluating the economy, efficiency and effectiveness with which Public Sector Organisations pursue their goals and objectives.
(j) Ensuring that costs are matched by at least equivalent benefits accruing therefrom.
(k) Providing the details of outstanding long-term commitments and financial obligations.
(l) Providing the means by which actual performance may be compared with the target set.
(m) Proffering solutions to the various bottlenecks and/or problems identified.

TEL: +233(0)548769918 /+233 (0) 501149296
Facebook Page: www.facebook.com/premiumicaglobal
Website: www.premiumonlinehub.com

1.8. TYPES OF INFORMATION PRODUCED BY PUBLIC SECTOR ORGANIZATIONS

The information produced by public sector organizations is by no means static. The information has been limited only to the needs of the user. In general, we may categorize the different types of information generated by public sector organizations as:

a. **Statutory information:** These are mandatory information that public sector organizations are required to produce by virtue of laws the established them.
The Financial Administration Regulations (FAR) compels Ministries, Departments, and
Agencies (MDAs) to produce monthly, quarterly and annual report of their finances and operations.

b. **Financing information:** These are information demanded by donors and other funding agencies to be produced by public sector organization according to a stipulated format.
This information focuses accountability, performance evaluation, and objectivity on public interest of the programmes.

c. **Planning information:** Planning by spending agencies in Ghana is based on a medium term expenditure framework (MTEF) which operates on cash basis normally for a period of three years. All spending agencies are expected to prepare their budgets on this planning model and report on the progress of their planning, programming and budgeting schemes.

d. **Budgetary information:** Budgetary information relates to the utilization of budgets as instruments of national economic management, communicating the resource constraints to spending departments, reducing gaps between planned and actual expenditures and achieving better control of public expenditures.

TEL: +233(0)548769918 /+233 (0) 501149296
Facebook Page: www.facebook.com/premiumicaglobal
Website: www.premiumonlinehub.com

e. **Control information:** Central control and monitoring of expenditure during a year is done by the treasury which provides regular reports on what has been spent and the estimated outturn of the year. Information for monitoring comes each month from the records of receipts and payments to the Consolidated Fund maintained by the treasury.

Control is exercised through cash limits that provide a system of government control of expenditure during the financial year.

1.9. USERS OF PUBLIC SECTOR FINANCIAL INFORMATION

Users	Information Needs
Donor Community	Whether organizational objects are pursued, and plans and targets are attainable
Media	How Government financial information impacts on all aspects of society
Economic Planners	Whether Government financial

TEL: +233(0)548769918 /+233 (0) 501149296
Facebook Page: www.facebook.com/premiumicaglobal
Website: www.premiumonlinehub.com

	information are adequate and received timely for planning purposes
Taxpayers	The consequences of Government spending, whether they will result in improvements in their living standards and/or increase taxation or inflation
Bankers and Lenders to Government	The financial position of government especially its ability to pay loans and interest thereon and Governments ability to borrow money.
Regulatory bodies	Whether Government spending meets legal requirements and whether financial controls are adhered to by spending agencies
Governments Economic Monitoring Authorities	Whether there is deficit or surplus on current accounts the quantum, and whether to borrow or mop up liquidity in the economy
Budget Analysts, Managerial Accountants and Investors	The trends of current monthly accounts and historical costs to help predict the future financial and economic position of the economy.
Revenue and other Finance	Monitor financial position of

TEL: +233(0)548769918 /+233 (0) 501149296
Facebook Page: www.facebook.com/premiumicaglobal
Website: www.premiumonlinehub.com

related Agencies of Government	government as a basis for structuring managerial and employees rewards system, such as bonuses for staff
Controller and Accountant-General	Uses financial reports to develop and maintain a management information system, capturing real time, the past, present and emerging development and behaviour patterns of various Government organizations.
Auditor-General	Whether Government accounts have been properly kept and records properly reported on
The Government Trade Unions	Require financial information to be used in salary negotiations.
Contractors and suppliers of goods	Are there enough money to pay for Government contracts?
Non-Governmental Organisations	Want to know key areas of the state that require social or economic intervention
The World bank, IMF, Multilateral and Bilateral Agencies and Foreign Governments	Wants to know the financial and economic performance of the country, where to assist, where to advice. They want to assess the effectiveness of spending on HIPC and Poverty Alleviation, the

TEL: +233(0)548769918 /+233 (0) 501149296
Facebook Page: www.facebook.com/premiumicaglobal
Website: www.premiumonlinehub.com

	sustainability of Fiscal Policies, net debt, net wealth, contingent claims against the Government and obligations for government pensions.
Private Sector Business	Whether Government borrowing from the commercial banks would affect their business, and whether they can do business with the Government?

2.0. THE CONCEPT OF PRIVATIZATION

Privatization refers to the process through which government or public owned institution (s) is sold to private individuals or entity (ies) or the government allowing private investors to take greater percentage of ownership and control of public institution (s).

2.0.1. Policy objectives of privatization

(i) To raise foreign exchange

(ii) To develop a domestic capital market

(iii) To motivate the private sector

(iv) To reduce the fiscal deficit

TEL: +233(0)548769918 /+233 (0) 501149296
Facebook Page: www.facebook.com/premiumicaglobal
Website: www.premiumonlinehub.com

(v) To improve the efficiency of the economy by encouraging private sector participation and investment

(vi) Government must not engage in commercial activities

2.0.2. Advantages Of Privatisation

1. Privatisation leads to lower prices and greater supply

2. It provides a one off cash boost for government to be used in other areas like schools, hospitals

3. The government cannot be a player and an empire

4. Private enterprises is more responsive to customer complaints and innovation

5. Competition in privatisation increase differentiation

6. Privatisation places the risk in the hands of business or private enterprises

7. Save Taxpayers money.

2.0.3. Disadvantages

TEL: +233(0)548769918 /+233 (0) 501149296
Facebook Page: www.facebook.com/premiumicaglobal
Website: www.premiumonlinehub.com

1. It is expensive and generate a lot of income in fees for specialist advisers e.g. Banks

2. Public monopolies have been turned into private monopolies with too little competition so consumers suffer.

3. The nationalised industries were sold off too quickly and too cheaply.

4. After purchase the buyers have sold off or closed down unprofitable parts of the business. E.g. Transport.

5. It creates unemployment e.g. layoffs after purchase.

6. Share ownership did not really happen as many small investors took their profits and did not buy anything else.

2.1. Comparison between Government Accounting and Private Sector Accounting

(a) The main objective of a commercial enterprise is to maximize profit while that of Government is to provide adequate welfare to the people at the reasonable costs.

(b) Government revenue is derived from the public in the form of taxation, fines, fees etc. whereas business concerns obtain their income principally from the sales of goods and services.

(c) In Government, financial transactions are recorded on 'cash basis' while in commercial organizations, it is on accrual basis.

(d) In Public Sector Accounting, tangible fixed assets such as land and building, plant and machinery are not shown in the balance sheet, whereas in private sector accounting these are reflected, showing the historical cost, accumulated depreciation and the net book value of each.

(e) In Public Sector Accounting, current assets such as stocks and debtors are not shown in the balance sheet. Debtors and creditors are not

TEL: +233(0)548769918 /+233 (0) 501149296
Facebook Page: www.facebook.com/premiumicaglobal
Website: www.premiumonlinehub.com

reckoned with until money is received or paid. The current assets and current liabilities are shown in private sector accounting system.

(f) In Government there is no Annual General Meeting of stakeholders/ shareholders, unlike the situation with commercial enterprises. What Government does is to hold public briefing on specific issues.

(g) In Public Sector Accounting, what operates substantially is fund accounting. However, in private sector accounting, the proprietary approach is adopted.

(h) Public Sector Accounting thrives rigidly on the budgetary approach, whereas in private sector accounting budgeting is embraced as a very potent control instrument.

TEL: +233(0)548769918 /+233 (0) 501149296
Facebook Page: www.facebook.com/premiumicaglobal
Website: www.premiumonlinehub.com

BASES OF PUBLIC SECTOR ACCOUNTING

INTRODUCTION

There are three bases under which the financial statements of a public sector enterprise are prepared and compiled. These are:
(a) The cash basis.
(b) The accrual basis.
(c) The commitment basis.

1.1. The Cash Basis
It is the basis of accounting under which revenue is recorded only when cash is received, and expenditure recognised only when cash is paid, irrespective of the fact that the transactions might have occurred in the previous accounting period.

1.1.1. Advantages of Cash Basis

The advantages of this basis include the following:

(a) It is simple to understand.

(b) It eliminates the existence of debtors and creditors.

(c) It permits easy identification of those who authorize payments and collect revenue.

(d) It allows for comparison between the amount provided in the budget and that actually spent.

(e) It saves time and is easy to operate.

(f) It permits the delegation of work in certain circumstances.

(g) The cost of fixed assets is written off in the year of purchase, resulting in fewer accounting entries.

TEL: +233(0)548769918 /+233 (0) 501149296
Facebook Page: www.facebook.com/premiumicaglobal
Website: www.premiumonlinehub.com

1.1.2. Disadvantages of the Cash Basis

(a) It takes unrealistic view of financial transactions as only the settlement of liabilities is recognised. For example, there are five stages through which a spending decision passes.

These are:

(i) Issue of order or contract for the supply of goods or services.

(ii) Supply of goods or services - acknowledgment of liability.

(iii) Settlement of the amount of the good or service received.

(iv) Consumption of value.

The cash basis of accounting records only stage (iii) while the accrual basis takes care of stages (ii), (iii) and (iv). The commitment basis records stages (i) to (iv).

(b) It does not provide for depreciation since assets are written off in the year of purchase.

(c) It does not convey an accurate picture of the financial affairs at the end of the year.

(d) The cash basis cannot be used for economic decisions as it tends to hide basic information. For example, some of the missing information relate to fixed assets, debtors and creditors.

(e) It does not accord with the 'matching concept.'

TEL: +233(0)548769918 /+233 (0) 501149296
Facebook Page: www.facebook.com/premiumicaglobal
Website: www.premiumonlinehub.com

1.2. Modified Cash Basis

Under this basis, the books of accounts are left open for a maximum of three months after the end of the year, so as to capture substantial amount of income or expenses relating to the year just ended.

1.3. Accrual Basis

Under this basis, revenue is recorded when earned and expenditure acknowledged as liabilities when known or benefits received, notwithstanding the fact that the receipts or payments of cash have taken place wholly or partly in other accounting periods.

1.3.1. Advantages of Accrual Basis

The advantages of this basis can be summarised as follows:

(a) It takes a realistic view of financial transactions.

(b) It reveals an accurate picture of the state of financial affairs at the end of the period.

(c) It could be used for both economic and investment decision-making as all parameters for performance appraisal are available.

(d) It aligns with the 'matching concept.'

(e) It makes allowances for the diminution in the value of assets used to generate the revenue of the enterprise.

1.3.2. Disadvantages of Accrual Basis

(a) It is very difficult to understand, especially by Non-Accountants.

(b) It does not permit easy delegation of work in certain circumstances.

TEL: +233(0)548769918 /+233 (0) 501149296
Facebook Page: www.facebook.com/premiumicaglobal
Website: www.premiumonlinehub.com

1.4. Modified Accrual Basis

This is the basis under which revenue is recorded when received and not earned while expenditure is recorded once its liability is incurred. It means that cash basis is used for recording revenue while accrual basis is adopted for expenditure.

The modified accrual basis operates as follows:

➢ Revenue is recorded when cash is received, except for:

(a) Revenue which is susceptible to accrual, and

(b) Revenue of a material amount which has not been received at the normal time it should.

➢ Expenditure is recorded on accrual basis, except in the cases of:

(a) Disbursements for inventory items which may be considered as expenditure at the time the items are utilised.

(b) Interest on long-term debt commonly accounted for in debt service funds, and recorded as expenditure on its due date

1.4.1. Ghana has recently adopted International Public Sector Accounting Standards (IPSAS).

Benefits of Accrual Basis (IPSAS)

- Better national/international comparability and consistency of financial information
- Transparency in government accounting and financial reporting which influences government's cost of refinancing
- Enhancement of accountability and oversight control
- Focus on public-sector-specific issues in financial reporting
- Better recognition of risks, opportunities, cost awareness and efficiency

TEL: +233(0)548769918 /+233 (0) 501149296
Facebook Page: www.facebook.com/premiumicaglobal
Website: www.premiumonlinehub.com

- Improved government finance statistical information
- Better decision-making and improvement of assets and liabilities management

1.5. Commitment Basis

It is a basis that records anticipated expenditure evidenced by a contract or a purchase order. In public sector financing, budgetary and accounting systems are closely related to the commitment basis.

1.5.1 Advantages of Commitment Basis

(a) A separate payment tabulation is available when required.

(b) Adjustment occurring when actual expenditure has been obtained does not affect the final accounts.

(d) It is an aid to financial control. A commitment is regarded as a char it takes a realistic view of financial transactions.

(e) It reveals an accurate picture of the state of financial affairs at the end of the period.

(f) It is used for both economic and investment decision-making, as all parameters or performance appraisals are available.

(g) It aligns with the 'matching concept.

(h) It makes allowance for the diminution in the value of assets employed to generate the revenue of the enterprise.

1.5.2. Disadvantages of Commitment Basis

(a) The system involves extra work. Actual figures have to be substituted for the commitment provisions to finally determine the running balances under the sub-heads of expenditure.

TEL: +233(0)548769918 /+233 (0) 501149296
Facebook Page: www.facebook.com/premiumicaglobal
Website: www.premiumonlinehub.com

(b) Over-expenditure is more under commitment basis in the expectation that Government may finally release fund to settle the legal obligations.

(c) At the year end, all commitments that are the subject of unfulfilled orders will have to be written back to reflect the exact picture of the transactions which took place during the year.

(d) Balances which ought to have lapsed in the Vote Book at the end of the year may be spent by issuing local purchase orders to exhaust the votes.

TEL: +233(0)548769918 /+233 (0) 501149296
Facebook Page: www.facebook.com/premiumicaglobal
Website: www.premiumonlinehub.com

REGULATORY FRAMEWORK OF PUBLIC SECTOR ACCOUNTING

INTRODUCTION

The regulatory framework refers to the regulations and Acts as well as directives and circulars about managing public resources or fund.

It has become almost like a maxim or a cardinal principle in every state that before any institution in the state can obtain government recognition or funding, if necessary it must be shrouded in governmental legality, quasi-legality or some government regulations. As such, almost every institution of the government is covered by laws and regulations.

While Laws are enabling acts, regulations on the other hand emanate from the Law and guide the day to day activities of the institution.

1.1. **The legal regulatory that regulates public sector financial operations in Ghana include:**
   - The 1992 constitution
   - The Financial Administration Act (2003) Act 654
   - The Financial Administration Regulation (2004) L.I. 1802
   - **The Intern**al Revenue Act
   - **The** Customs Excise and Preventive Act
   - The Bank of Ghana Act
   - The District Assembly Common Fund Act
   - Procurement Agency Act (2003) Act 663
   - Audit Service Act (2000) Act 584
   - Internal Audit Agency Act (2003) Act 658
   - Local Government Act
   - Any other regulation that the parliament may enact from time to time.

TEL: +233(0)548769918 /+233 (0) 501149296
Facebook Page: www.facebook.com/premiumicaglobal
Website: www.premiumonlinehub.com

1.2. Role of Regulatory Authorities

1.2.1. THE EXECUTIVE (Office Of The President /Cabinet)

Decisions on government policies with regards to financial outlay are taken by the office of the President together with the Cabinet representing the executive arm of government.

In the course of making decisions with financial implications, the executive arm of government must exercise careful control about appropriations. This is because; the decisions must be approved by parliament.

1.2.2. PARLIAMENTARY CONTROL (Legislative Arm Of Government)

According to the rules in the 1992 constitution of Ghana, no revenue shall be levied or expenditure incurred except as authorised by parliament.

Parliamentary financial control is exercised in three different phases namely; *appropriation*, *audit* and review by *public accounts committee*.

a. Appropriation

Before parliament approves the utilisation of public funds it follows certain basic rules of financial controls, namely;

- Appropriate budget authority
- Appropriate budget period
- Appropriate budget classification
- Appropriate budget reallocations approved by the MoFEP (Minister of Finance and Economic Planning)
- Value for money
- Payment are for purposes for which they are intended
- Documents supporting expenditure are valid and appropriate
- Relevant rules and regulations pertaining to the expenditure will be adhered to
- Expenditure will be subject to internal and external audit scrutiny.

TEL: +233(0)548769918 /+233 (0) 501149296
Facebook Page: www.facebook.com/premiumicaglobal
Website: www.premiumonlinehub.com

b. Audit Control

To ensure that the rules on appropriation of public funds are followed, parliament has the power to approve the appointment of the Auditor General to examine both the accounts of the executive arm of government and all spending units *(Metropolitan, Municipal and District Assemblies – MMDAs & Ministries Departments and Agencies – MDAs)* and also to assist it to ascertain that rules governing procedures on expenditure and principles of public sector accounting have been applied. The Auditor General is also obliged to report to parliament any non-adherence to the law and also draw the attention of parliament to instances of wasteful expenditures, losses, malfeasance, etc.

c. Review by the Public Accounts Committee

The public accounts committee does a thorough study of the audited accounts of the government which is submitted to its office. It examines breaches of the law or waste, and summons MDAs and MMDAs to account for their stewardship.

➢ Public Accounts Committee

For completeness, Article 187 (6) of the Constitution enjoins Parliament first to debate the report of the Auditor-General, and second, to appoint where necessary, in the public interest, a committee to deal with any matters arising from its study of the report. Parliament therefore requires the Auditor-General to perform its oversight function over the executive use of public resources. This committee in parliament examines the Auditor-General's report together with the Public Accounts in detail and sort "grill" departmental heads on financial authorization, compliance and avoidance of gross extravagance.

However, invariably, the committee does not seem to have power to surcharge or dismiss but it can question and reprimand and direct the implementation of recommendations by the Auditor-General; as such "tough skinned" public officials are not perturbed by their activities.

TEL: +233(0)548769918 /+233 (0) 501149296
Facebook Page: www.facebook.com/premiumicaglobal
Website: www.premiumonlinehub.com

1.2.2.1. Reasons for Parliamentary failure to control expenditure

(i) Political stands of Parliamentarians supporting their parties

(ii) Lack of resources to operate efficiently

(iii) Lack of training or technical skills to deal with the issue

(iv) Self benefits from the non-control

(v) Late submission of the Auditor-General's report to Parliament

(vi) Ministers doubling as Parliamentarians

(vii) Lack of legal framework to deal with issues

1.2.3. The Controller and Accountant General's Department (CAGD)

1.2.3.1 Statutory Duties
Section 3 (Financial Administration Act, 2003) Act 654

1. Responsible to the minister of finance for the custody, safety and integrity of the consolidated fund and other public funds under his care;

2. Responsible for compilation and management of the consolidated fund and other public funds;

3. He is the chief accounting officer of the government responsible for keeping, rendering and publishing statements of public accounts as required by law;

4. He is the chief advisor to the minister of finance and the government on accountancy matters;

5. He approves departmental accounting instructions and promotes the development of efficient accounting systems within departments;

TEL: +233(0)548769918 /+233 (0) 501149296
Facebook Page: www.facebook.com/premiumicaglobal
Website: www.premiumonlinehub.com

6. He is responsible for receipt, secure custody of public moneys payable into the consolidated fund.

7. He authorizes the opening of bank accounts of MDAs and MMDAs

8. In consultation with the auditor general, he specifies for departments, the accounting basis, policies and classification system to ensure proper system of accounting;

1.2.3.2. Regulatory Control Duties
The regulatory control duties of the controller and accountant general in public financial management are as follow:

- Relating each spending department's requirements to the economic resources estimated to be available and to the total claims on them;
- Keeping public expenditure within total resources for the year;
- Advising departments on economic and financial policy, via treasury circulars;
- Controlling government expenditures through co-ordination and monitoring operations of MDAs and MMDAs;
- Considering matters covered by the reports of the public accounts committee of parliament and co-operating to improve financial control;
- Initiating programmes to improve financial management, including the provision and guidance improvements, in public sector accounting.

1.2.4.   The Auditor General

1.2.4.1. Statutory Duties:

1. Section 11, Audit Service Act, 2000 (Act 548)

The public accounts of Ghana and of all public offices, including the courts, the central and local government administrations, of the

TEL: +233(0)548769918 /+233 (0) 501149296
Facebook Page: www.facebook.com/premiumicaglobal
Website: www.premiumonlinehub.com

universities and public institutions of like nature, of a public corporation or other body or organization established by an act of parliament shall be audited and reported on by the auditor general.

2. Section 13- Examination of Accounts

The auditor-general shall examine in such manner as he thinks necessary the public and other government accounts and shall ascertain whether in his opinion:

a. The accounts have been properly kept;

b. All public monies have been fully accounted for and rules and procedures applicable are sufficient to secure an effective check on the assessment, collection and proper allocation of the revenue;

c. Monies have been expended for the purpose for which they were appropriated and the expenditures have been made as authorized;

d. Essential records are maintained and the rules and procedures applied are sufficient to safeguard and control public property; and

e. Programmes and activities have been taken with due regard to economy, efficiency and effectiveness in relation to the resources utilized and results achieved.

1.2.4.2. Other Duties

Section 12 – audit of foreign exchange transactions
Section 14 – audit of statutory corporations;
Section 15 – examination of annual statement of public accounts prepared by controller and accountant general;
Section 16 – submission of special audit report to parliament;
Section 17 – disallowance of surcharge.

TEL: +233(0)548769918 /+233 (0) 501149296
Facebook Page: www.facebook.com/premiumicaglobal
Website: www.premiumonlinehub.com

1.2.5. THE MINISTER OF FINANCE AND ECONOMIC PLANNING

Roles of the Minister of Finance and Economic Planning (MoFEP)

- Develops and implements macro-economic and fiscal policy framework for the country;
- Supervises and monitors the finances of the country;
- Co-ordinates international and inter - governmental financial and fiscal relation;
- Advises the government on the total resources to be allocated to individual programmes and activities within the sector;
- Develop preliminary ceilings by allocating total resources between sectors on the basis of government priorities. These ceiling are approved by Cabinet.
- Conducts budgets hearings, reviews and finalises budget statement;
- Presents to parliament, the fiscal policy of the government and a statement of the current and projected state of the economy (budget), not less than once a year.

1.2.6. The financial duties of a head of department are:

(1) Management and operate the department's accounting systems, so as to ensure the accountability of all officers transacting business and facilitate the efficient discharge of such business

(2) To ensure that the department's accounting system has been approved by the Controller and Accountant-General in consultation with the Auditor-General.

(3) Secure the efficient and effective use of appropriations under departmental control within the ambit of government policy and in compliance with any enactment or of instructions issued under the authority of any enactment

(4) Secure the due and proper collection of government revenue collectable by department within the terms of any enactment or of instructions issued or approved by the Controller and Accountant-General

TEL: +233(0)548769918 /+233 (0) 501149296
Facebook Page: www.facebook.com/premiumicaglobal
Website: www.premiumonlinehub.com

(5) Request, commit, order, receive and make payments for goods and services within the funds appropriated to the department and in accordance with this regulations and any other enactment

(6) Receive and order the disbursement of any trust moneys for which the head of department has been appointed as administering authority by or under any enactment or agreement

(7) Manage and reconcile the bank accounts authorised for the department by the Controller and Accountant-General

(8) Preserve in good order and secure the economical use of all equipment and stores used by the department

(9) Transact any other financial business for which the head of department is made responsible, by or under any enactment in accordance with the requirement of the enactment or instructions issued or approved by the Minister

(10) Compile and maintain assets register of the department as determined by the Controller and Accountant-General

(11) Appear before the Public Accounts Committee to give any explanations required by the committee in respect of annual departmental accounts

(12) Answer questions raised by the auditor-General in respect of financial transactions and accounts of the department

(13) Prepare, sign and submit within three months after the year end, to the Minister, auditor-General and Accountant-General, annual departmental accounts in the form prescribed by the controller and Accountant-General in consultation with the auditor-General.

TEL: +233(0)548769918 /+233 (0) 501149296
Facebook Page: www.facebook.com/premiumicaglobal
Website: www.premiumonlinehub.com

1.3. FACTORS TO BE CONSIDERED BY GOVERNMENT TO EXERCISE THE SOVEREIGN AUTHORITY OF THE STATE

The sovereign authority of the state is the power of the government to tax, borrow and create money to meet the aspirations of the Ghanaian public and raise their standard of living.

The following are the factors that the government should consider in exercising this authority are as follows:

The four factors are:

1. Objectives of the state (vision of government)
2. Fiscal policy (taxation etc.)
3. Monetary policy (inflation, money supply etc.)
4. The estimates (costing of activities)

1. **The objectives of the state**: This varies from period to period and depends on which government is in power. The broad national objectives are captured in the Directive Principles of state policy in the nation's constitution a decade ago; the objective was vision 2020, a brand policy to move Ghana to the middle income status. This objective was to move the timeframe to 2015 with the launch of Growth and Poverty Reduction Strategy. At present there is a new policy direction with four thematic areas:

- Investment in human capital.

- Expansion of infrastructure.

- Job creation.

- Transparent and accountable governance.

2. **Government fiscal policy** is the term used for the government's policy of taxation, payments and financing deficit gaps. The government raises through taxation to carry out its program. It is the amount through taxation is insufficient, for the budgeted program then other means of raising funds are used to meet the deficit. This is normally achieved by borrowing on the local market by means of treasury bills or borrowing

TEL: +233(0)548769918 /+233 (0) 501149296
Facebook Page: www.facebook.com/premiumicaglobal
Website: www.premiumonlinehub.com

externally from multi-donor institutions like IMF and World Bank or look for grants or donations.

3. **The supply of money in the economy** determines economic activity and the prevailing price level. Attention is therefore focused on bank of Ghana and its attempt to regulate the money supply of the country. Economists believe that if the supply increases beyond the normal increase in economic activity (about 4 -5 %p.a.) inflationary spending ensues.

Similarly, if the growth in the money supply is below the level of economic activity recessionary tendencies increases.

4. **The annual estimates** are prepared in quantitative terms using the government chart of accounts and MTEF principles of planning and programming.

From the annual estimates government is able to know.

- Projected revenue and expenditure for the year.
- The allocation of funds for various functions and program including administration, service and investments.
- Whether it will have surplus or deficit in its current accounts and to plan whether to borrow or invest funds.
- And to decide on the appropriate level and structure of public debts.

TEL: +233(0)548769918 /+233 (0) 501149296
Facebook Page: www.facebook.com/premiumicaglobal
Website: www.premiumonlinehub.com

PUBLIC SECTOR ACCOUNTING SYSTEMS

1.1. Introduction

The public sector accounting system is actually a series of systems and subsystems that track the financial activities of government and government agencies.
Financial management of the Government is concerned with budgetary and financial operations of both individual departments and agencies and the Government as a whole.

1.2. Objectives of Public sector accounting systems

- It enhance full disclosure of the financial results of department and agency activities;
- To the enable the production of adequate financial information needed for departments and agency management purposes;
- For the effective control over and accountability for all funds, property, and other assets for which each department and agency is responsible;
- It gives a reliable accounting reports to serve as the basis for preparation and supporting of department and agency budget requests to control the execution of the budget and to provide financial information;
- It enhances a suitable integration of department and agency accounting with the central accounting and reporting operations of the Treasury Department.

1.3. Techniques for Accounting in the Public Sector

In the public sector, techniques of accounting depend on financial decisions which are usually formulated on the basis of the information generated from the accounting systems, and also on the type of fund operated.

The techniques may be summarized as follows:

TEL: +233(0)548769918 /+233 (0) 501149296
Facebook Page: www.facebook.com/premiumicaglobal
Website: www.premiumonlinehub.com

1. **Vote Accounting** It is concerned with the receipt, custody, disbursement, and transfer of public and trust monies as required by law.
2. **Fund Accounting** A fund is an independent accounting entity and must be accounted for using a separately identified set of accounts in such a way that it is possible to identify the specific assets and liabilities that represent the balance on the fund.

➢ **Reasons / uses of Fund Accounting**

i.   It allows for the demonstration of fiduciary stewardship. That is, it shows that resources have been handled in a proper way through proper procedures.

ii.   It assists in reaching fund's objectives based on policies and program, requirements of its implementation, monitory and evaluation

iii.   It provides rules of accounting and responsibility of stewards who operate the funds.

iv.   In the public sector, diversity of functions and restrictions on how certain resources may be used makes it necessary to focus attention on individual areas of operation and to segregate resources provided for specific purpose. This is made possible by the use of Fund Accounting.

v.   Financial reporting on government is seen as a series of reporting units and Fund Accounting allows some flexibility in defining reporting units as entities as entities within an explicit frame work of controls.

3. **Project Accounting** It involves controlling, measuring and analysing the activities and lifeline of a specific project.

4. **Donor Support Accounting** This is concerned with receipts, custody and disbursement of the financial donation of donor or support organizations.

TEL: +233(0)548769918 /+233 (0) 501149296
Facebook Page: www.facebook.com/premiumicaglobal
Website: www.premiumonlinehub.com

5. **Environmental Accounting**

Environmental Accounting is the process incorporating environmental issues into the government financial reporting systems.
Environmental Accounting is often referred to as Green Accounting which incorporates environmental assets and their source and side functions into national accounts.

➤ **Reasons for considering Environmental Accounting**

i.   Possible revenue generation may off-set environmental cost.

ii.   Environmental cost and benefits may be over-looked or hidden in overhead accounts.

iii.   Possible significant reduction or elimination of environmental costs

iv.   Benefitting from environmental products and services to the citizens

v.   Can support the development and running of an overall Environmental Management Systems (EMS) which may be required by regulation for some types of businesses.

vi.   Positive impact on human health by improving environmental conditions.

vii.   May result in more accurate costing or pricing of products and more environmental desired processes.

TEL: +233(0)548769918 /+233 (0) 501149296
Facebook Page: www.facebook.com/premiumicaglobal
Website: www.premiumonlinehub.com

1.4. Benefits of the accounting systems

- Formulate the general objectives of the agency and co-ordinate the policies of individual's financial needs of the various units.

- Relate each spending units requirements to the economic resources estimated to be available and the total claims to them.

- Keep expenditure within total resources of the year.

- Advise management and each unit about financial control measures of the agency.

1.5. Chart of Accounts

Definition of CoA

CoA is a structured set of codes that provides a framework for Recording, Classifying, and Organising Budget Data and Accounting Transactions into Reports and Statements. It provides various perspectives of financial transactions and facilitates budgetary controls.

This technique of revenue and expenditure classification is very necessary to show the complex nature of government or public sector accounting. On the chart of accounts MDAs and MMDAs are used as expenditure heads and it is possible to trace revenue collected into the Consolidated Fund to its primary source.

1.5.1. Segments of the harmonised CoA

a. **Institution Segment-** This segment is used for coding an Institutional Unit which stands as an economic entity. An institutional unit as defined in the GFS 2001 Manual "is an economic entity that is capable, in its own right, of owning assets, incurring liabilities, and engaging in economic activities and in transactions with other entities. These entities should be treated as separate government units if they maintain full

TEL: +233(0)548769918 /+233 (0) 501149296
Facebook Page: www.facebook.com/premiumicaglobal
Website: www.premiumonlinehub.com

sets of accounts, own goods or assets in their own right, engage in non-market activities for which they are held accountable at law, and are able to incur liabilities and enter into contracts."

b. **Funding Segment** - The Funding segment provides a means to track the source of funding for expenditures within a consolidated reporting scheme. Expenditures are assigned against the appropriate funding code, independent from the organizational or program structure.

c. **Functional of Government (COFOG) Segment** – This segment provide coding for functional classification of expense to provide a strategic view of the allocation of budget resources between different sectors of the economy. This is based on the United Nations Classification of Functions of Government (COFOG). It is a detailed classification of the functions, or socioeconomic objectives (e.g., health, education, defence, etc.), that Government units aim to achieve through various programmes.

d. **Organisational Segment** - The Organizational segment provides the basis for establishing the responsibilities for the day-to-day administration of government business. The structure of the organizational hierarchy is reflected in the series of codes for ministries, departments and agencies (Cost Centres/ Spending Units) reporting under the Sector Ministries.

e. **Program and Sub-programme Segments** – These segments provide the basis for recording transactions associated with a specific program or sub-program that is operating under an organizational unit

f. **Activity Segment** – This segment provides classification of various activities related to specific programmes, sub-programmes or outputs.

TEL: +233(0)548769918 /+233 (0) 501149296
Facebook Page: www.facebook.com/premiumicaglobal
Website: www.premiumonlinehub.com

g. **Location Segment** – Provides geographical location of an institution, organisation, programme, etc. based on established political and administrative districts of Ghana.

h. **The Natural Accounts segment** – This is an Economic Classification which provides the basis for recording specific activity by the kind of transactions by which the Government performs its functions. This segment provides classification and coding for revenue, expenditure, liabilities, etc.

1.5.2. **Uses of harmonized chart of accounts may also he explained as follows**:

a. Harmonization of accounts of MDAs and MMDAs;

b. Uniform classification of accounts in public financial management;

c. Control of accounts in public financial management;

d. Tracking of revenue and expenditure in public financial management;

e. Efficiency and effectiveness in budgetary resource allocation; and

f. Design of audit trail

TEL: +233(0)548769918 /+233 (0) 501149296
Facebook Page: www.facebook.com/premiumicaglobal
Website: www.premiumonlinehub.com

SOURCES OF GOVERNMENT REVENUE

1.1. Introduction

It is the task of government to provide essential services to the community – the maintenance of law and order, building of roads and ports, schools and hospitals and countless other activities necessary to the modern nation. But in order to provide these services, the government must be able to finance them by ensuring that there is a sufficient flow of money into its hands to enable it to pay for the work it must undertake.

Over the past decades, the financial system of central government has become increasingly complex. This is because, not only has the amount of money flowing in and out of the public treasury every year increased tremendously, but it flows in from many more different sources, and it is disbursed for very greater variety of activities.

Revenue constitutes the ordinary income of government, being composed of taxation (the major source of revenue) and earnings (charges raised by government departments for services rendered to the public, rents received for the lease of government lands or building, interest on investments by the government and so on). **This is the inflow of money into the central treasury to finance expenditure.**

1.2. **Revenue** is an increase in net worth resulting from a transaction.
There are four main sources of revenue:

- Taxes and other compulsory transfer imposed by government units

- Property income derived from the ownership of assets

- Sale of goods and services

- Voluntary transfers received from other units (Grants)

TEL: +233(0)548769918 /+233 (0) 501149296
Facebook Page: www.facebook.com/premiumicaglobal
Website: www.premiumonlinehub.com

1.3. Categorisation of Revenue

i.   **Tax Revenue**: This forms the dominant share of revenue for many government units and is composed of compulsory transfers to the government sector. Certain compulsory transfers such as fines, penalties, and most social security contributions are excluded from **tax revenue.** It is further re-categorised into Direct Tax and Indirect Tax.

Tax Revenue sources include the following:

a.   **Direct Tax:**

Direct Taxes are taxes amount earned by individuals and companies, such as income tax, corporate tax and export duty. It also includes Capital Gains Tax and Gift tax.

b.   **Indirect Tax:**

This is a tax which is not paid directly by the person who suffers or bears the burden. This type of tax is put on goods and services that are bought and consumed by individuals. They include taxes on general goods and services, excises, customs and other imports, taxes on Export and levies.

ii.   **Non- tax revenue:** All other forms of revenue apart from taxes are referred to as Non-tax revenue. Example may include grants, loans, royalties, sale of goods and services, etc.

a.   **Grants** are non-compulsory transfers received by government or government units from international

TEL: +233(0)548769918 /+233 (0) 501149296
Facebook Page: www.facebook.com/premiumicaglobal
Website: www.premiumonlinehub.com

organizations and other developed countries like United Kingdom, America, China, France, among others.

b. **Property income, sales of goods and services, fines, penalties and other revenues.**

1.4. BREAKDOWN OF REVENUE SOURCES

Below are the necessary contributions as captured in the 1992 final accounts of the Consolidated Fund:

Taxes on International Transactions	17%
Value Added Tax	28%
Taxes on Personal Income	28%
Taxes on Domestic goods	13%
HIPIC	5%
Grants	5%
Non-tax Revenue	2%
Divestiture	0.0%

1.5. Sources of MDAs and MMDAs Revenue

In Ghana, MDAs and MMDAs sources of funds may be grouped into:

a. **Government of Ghana Transfer:**

These are transfers from the Consolidated Fund and other government units and include:

- *Central Government – Government of Ghana paid Salaries*

TEL: +233(0)548769918 /+233 (0) 501149296
Facebook Page: www.facebook.com/premiumicaglobal
Website: www.premiumonlinehub.com

- *Ceded Revenue*
- *School Feeding Program/HIV/AIDS, etc.*
- *DACF Direct transfers – capital development projects*

b. **Internally Generated Fund or Revenue:**

Generation, management and utilization of IGFs are anchored on several pieces of legislation notably:

- *Articles 174 & 179 of the 1992 Republic Constitution of Ghana*

- *MDA (Retention) of Funds Act, Act 753 of 2007;*
- *Fees and Charges Miscellaneous Provisions Act, Act 793;*

- *Fees and Charges (Amendment) Instrument of 2011; L.I 1986;*
- *Part III of the Financial Administration Act, Act 654 of 2003; and*

- *Part II of the Financial Administration Regulation of 2004.*

IGFs

i.   *Taxes on property*
ii.   *Taxes on goods and services*
iii. *Property income*
iv.   *Sales of goods and services*
v.   *Fines, penalties and forfeits.*

1.5.1. Ways to improve Internally Generated Funds (IGFs) of Local Government

a. Recruitment of quality and competent revenue staff

b. Outsourcing of revenue allocation to competent commission collectors

c. Setting of revenue targets for revenue collectors

d. Proper supervision of revenue staff to prevent revenue leakages of records

e. Rotation of revenue staff to prevent collusion

f. Accurate data collection to ascertain improved revenue forecast

g. Education, sensitization and demonstration to general public that revenue collected will be used judiciously for the benefit of the community.

h. Periodic valuation and revaluation of taxable properties to ensure proper property rate collection.

i. Motivation of revenue staff including periodic awards to induce productivity.

j. Improving the monitoring of revenue collection

1.6. Causes of failure to meet revenue targets

1. Corruption on the part of the staff of the revenue collecting Agencies.

2. Improper records keeping by the Tax Payers

3. Lack of motivation

4. Revenue collection agencies not integrated

5. Difficulty in locating Tax Payers in the informal sector

6. Lack of logistics for tax collection

7. Lack of training or revenue collecting officers.

TEL: +233(0)548769918 /+233 (0) 501149296
Facebook Page: www.facebook.com/premiumicaglobal
Website: www.premiumonlinehub.com

1.7. Sources of Government Domestic Borrowing

i. **Issue of securities**: - these are government borrowings through the issue of Treasury bills, Notes and Bonds on the domestic market.

ii. **Commercial Banks & Financial Institutions**: - these are long term loans borrowed from the domestic banking sector and non-banking sector like SSNIT.

iii. **Domestic Supplier Credit**: - these include the issue of letters of credit to local contractors to enable the contractors access credit facilities from banks. The contractors honour their obligations when the government pays them.

iv. **Advances from Bank of Ghana**: - these are monies advanced to the government by the Bank from their reserves. The advances are refunded when the government has sufficient revenue.

TEL: +233(0)548769918 /+233 (0) 501149296
Facebook Page: www.facebook.com/premiumicaglobal
Website: www.premiumonlinehub.com

GOVERNMENT EXPENDITURE AND PAYMENT PROCESS

1.1. Introduction

The public sector is the largest single organization, employer and spender in Ghana.

In Ghana, public expenditure could be defined as expenses, commitments, obligations and transfer payments of government. Although there is a closure of public accounts at the end of each calendar year, public expenditure never ceases and continues from year to year.

1.2. The main composition of public expenditure

The main composition of public expenditure in Ghana may be outlined as follows:

ITEM	PERCENTAGE (%)
Personal Emolument	36
Social security fund	3%
Pension and Gratuity	3%
Administration	24%
Service	9%
Investment	4%
District Assemble Common Fund	7.5%
Petroleum Related Fund	4
Ghana Education Trust Fund	2

TEL: +233(0)548769918 /+233 (0) 501149296
Facebook Page: www.facebook.com/premiumicaglobal
Website: www.premiumonlinehub.com

Road and Non- Road Arrears	3
Public Debt Interest	3
Utility Price Subsidies	-

1.2.1. Description of Expenditure Items

a. Transfer for salaries, wages and other benefits

These include salaries of public officers on established posts and non-established post, contract appointments, daily-rated employees and officers on probation, social security contributions and miscellaneous allowances.

b. **Administration expenses**

c. **Service expenses.** These are expenditure incurred by public organization in carrying out their mandate to achieve their objectives.

d. **Investment Expenses:** They are capital expenditures for which the benefits may be enjoyed by the organization for more than one accounting period.

e. **Pension and Gratuity**

f. **District Assembly Common fund:** These are grants paid by the Central Government every quarter of the year to MMDAs as a financial support for their planned programs.

g. **Petroleum Related Fund:** These are costs related to imports of crude oil brought into the country for refining purposes borne by

TEL: +233(0)548769918 /+233 (0) 501149296
Facebook Page: www.facebook.com/premiumicaglobal
Website: www.premiumonlinehub.com

the government. They include costs on foreign currency exchanges, subsidies and others.

h. **Ghana Education Trust Fund**
i. **Roan and Non-Road Trust Fun**

j. **Public Debt Interest:** These are regular and periodic payments of interest charges made by the government to service the country's debts.

1.3. Mode of Funding Institutional Commitments

i. **Appropriation:** The commitment of greater number of government institutions are funded by appropriations.

   An appropriation is the approval by parliament of annual or supplementary budget allocations to reflect expenditure commitments classified under programmes or, activities namely; heads, sub-heads, objectives, outputs, items and sub-items.

   Appropriations are used only for the purposes intended and within the limits set by the classification in the approved estimates of the government institution.

ii. **Local Revenue**
   Metropolitan, Municipal and District Assemblies are empowered by law to raise local taxes to finance their operations. These include rates, fees and fines, land, licenses and rents.

iii. **Transfers of salaries, wages and other benefits to MMDSs**
   TEL: +233(0)548769918 /+233 (0) 501149296
   Facebook Page: www.facebook.com/premiumicaglobal
   Website: www.premiumonlinehub.com

The government also funds public institutions by paying remuneration in cash or in kind, such as clothes, boots, shoes, to an employee in return for work done.

iv. **Supply of Fixed Capital, Goods and Services**

These include the government office premises, sanitation equipment, fire tenders, hospital ambulances, police vehicles and other capital items.

v. **Interest charges, payment of VAT, Port duties, etc.**
The government sometimes pays port charges, VAT and settles interest payments for government units which may not have funds in their budgetary allocations to settle these bills.
vi. Subsidies
vii. Grants
viii. Revenue Retention
ix. Donor Funds
x. Government Borrowing and Bank Guarantees
xi. Government lending

1.6. Government Payment Process

Payments are made through the Treasuries either by cash or direct debits. The procedures for payments involve the distinct organizations or regulatory bodies, namely; the Ministry of Finance and Economic Planning (MoFEP), the Controller and Accounting Generals Department (CAGD) and Ministries, Departments and Agencies (MDAs).

Public Expenditures can further be grouped into two namely Statutory and Non- statutory expenditures.

TEL: +233(0)548769918 /+233 (0) 501149296
Facebook Page: www.facebook.com/premiumicaglobal
Website: www.premiumonlinehub.com

1.6.1. Statutory Expenditure

These expenditures are paid out of the consolidated fund but do not require parliamentary approval. These expenditures are also known as Charged Expenditure. They include the following:

- Pension and Gratuity
- District Assembly Common Fund
- Petroleum Related Fund
- Ghana Education Trust Fund
- Road Fund
- HIPC expenditure
- Public Debt Interest

1.6.2. Non Statutory Expenditure:

These are expenditures which require Parliamentary approval in a form of debate before authorization is given for such expenditure. These are also known as *Discretionary Expenditures or Voted Expenditures.*

They include the following:

- Compensation of Employees
- Use of Goods and Services
- Fixed assets
- Among others

TEL: +233(0)548769918 /+233 (0) 501149296
Facebook Page: www.facebook.com/premiumicaglobal
Website: www.premiumonlinehub.com

1.7. **The payment procedures are as follows**:

Ministry of Finance and Economic Planning (MoFEP)

Under items 1-4:

The MDAs prepare annual work plans based on the budget guidelines issued by the MoFEP. The MoFEP then issues monthly cash ceilings to MDAs, principal accounts holders (spending officers).

The MDAs advice the CAGD on their disaggregated cash ceiling to their divisions and units. Upon this the CAGD issues monthly Warrant cash ceiling for items 1 & 2 by the 15th of month preceding the month, disaggregated into National, Regional and District levels.

MDAs then issue monthly divisional Warrant to their units and copies are sent to the CAGD and also the:
MDA – Principal accounts holder (Spending officer)
District – Principal Account's holder (Spending officer)

For items 3 & 4 MDAs are required to apply for specific warrants from MoFEP before CAGD also issues them with warrants.

After the CAGD has issued the warrant it then issues, monthly bank transfer advice equal to the monthly warrants to Bank of Ghana (BoG), for the transfer of cash from the main **Consolidated Fund** to the sub-consolidated fund special bank account of the Ministry (HQ), RCC and the District.

Copies are sent to:

National, RCC, district treasury (Director of Finance, Regional Finance Director and District officer)

MDA – Principal accounts holder (Spending officer) receives transcripts of the spending unit warrants from: National, RCC, district treasury (Director of Finance, Regional Finance Director and District officer).

TEL: +233(0)548769918 /+233 (0) 501149296
Facebook Page: www.facebook.com/premiumicaglobal
Website: www.premiumonlinehub.com

Under item 3 & 4

Based on specific warrants received from MoFEP, CAGD prepares bank transfer latter to BoG for the transfer of cash into the sub-consolidated fund account of the national, regional and district levels. Copies are sent to MDA – Principal accounts holder (Spending officer).

1.8. Warrant

A warrant is an order drawn authorising payment to a designated payee (MDAs/MMDAs).

1.8.1.   A warrant is an important document because:

- It gives the spending officer the authority to request that payments are made;
- It lets the spending officer know how much he can spend;
- It shows that sufficient funds remain in the cote to cover expenditure;
- It „rations" the amount of the vote that can be spent during the period;
- It determines how funds should be used (by specifying an account number);
- It limits the amount a spending officer can spend.

TEL: +233(0)548769918 /+233 (0) 501149296
Facebook Page: www.facebook.com/premiumicaglobal
Website: www.premiumonlinehub.com

1.8.2. Requirement for Issuing Warrants

Warrants shall be issued based on submission of MDA Consolidated work/cash Plan to Ministry of Finance.

- Authorization 1 – National Warrant: Issued by the Minister of finance to the Director of Budget.

- Authorization 2 – Ministry Warrant: Issued by the Director of Budget to transfer approved budget to MDAs.

- Authorization 3 – Department Warrants: Issued by Ministries to its Departments.

Authorization Levels of General Warrant

- Authorization 4 – Divisional Warrants: Issued by Departments to its Divisions.

- Authorization 5 Spending Units Warrants: Issued by Divisions to its Cost Centres where spending takes place.

Note: Budget can only be committed at Authorization 5.

Processing General Warrant

- All warrants received by MDAs should be lodged at servicing treasury.
- Servicing Treasuries should immediately enter particulars of warrants in the Vote service ledger.

TEL: +233(0)548769918 /+233 (0) 501149296
Facebook Page: www.facebook.com/premiumicaglobal
Website: www.premiumonlinehub.com

1.9. Methods of Controlling Public Expenditure:

Government at various times adopts mechanism for controlling public sector expenditures, prominent among them are discussed below:

- **Freezing of Votes:**

Sometimes the Government may instruct the Treasury to cease the disbursement of public funds for a period. This allows Government to build up enough revenue to meet its commitment.

- **Quarterly Limits:**

Approved votes for the financial year are released quarterly instead of yearly. This allows the Government to limit expenditure to expected quarterly revenues.

- **Warrants:**

Funds released by the MoFEP and the CAG to MDAs are subsequently disbursed through the use of warrants. This procedure enables the MoFEP and the CAG to disburse funds within limits of the available revenue.

- **Across the Board Cuts:**

When the Government monitors expenditure against its budgeted revenue and revenue received has fallen far below target, the government may impose a mandatory cut on all expenditures by a certain percentage.

2. Expenditure Control:

Expenditure control could be defined as the strings of coordinated actions which have to be taken to ensure that all expenditure are 'wholly', 'necessarily', 'reasonably' and 'exclusively' incurred for the purpose for which they are meant.

TEL: +233(0)548769918 /+233 (0) 501149296
Facebook Page: www.facebook.com/premiumicaglobal
Website: www.premiumonlinehub.com

2.0. Types of Expenditure Control

2.1. The Executive:

The President in order to satisfy the provisions of the Constitution also appoints a Cabinet Committee on Estimates, to advise him on the contemplated policy measures. The policy measures contemplated are then transmitted to the Budget Department in the Presidency. This development in turn leads to the issuance of guidelines on the preparation of the Budget. As a result, effective supervision is exercised on all the Agencies involved in budget operation.

2.2. Legislative Control

The concept of legislative control of public expenditure has to do with the various measures that Parliament can use for purposes of controlling public expenditure.

The 1992 Constitution establishes the Parliamentary Authority over public funds and their uses.

Parliament achieves such financial control over public expenditure and revenue through the following:

a. **Public Finance Committee:**

This committee is responsible for the receipt of the Finance Bill, Budgets and Proposal of government for the consideration of parliament.

b. **Appropriation Committee:**

This committee is responsible for the passing of the Appropriation Act for the purposes of authorizing the Budget after examination by various sub-committees.

TEL: +233(0)548769918 /+233 (0) 501149296
Facebook Page: www.facebook.com/premiumicaglobal
Website: www.premiumonlinehub.com

c. **Examination Sub- Committee:**

These are sub-committees of Parliament that are responsible for the examination of individual estimates of the organizations.

d. **Public Accounts Committee:**

This committee receives the Public Accounts, examines and debates its contents and submits its report (s) in the form of its findings and recommendations to the whole House.

e. **The Audit Service:**

This institution is responsible for the examination of public accounts to attest to the use of the various public funds as were sanctioned by the Parliament at the beginning of the year.

The limitations of Legislative Control have already been discussed under the Regulatory Responsibilities of Parliament.

2.3. Ministry of Finance Control

The MDAs have to apply to the Minister of Finance for funds to pay for services. The tradition is that, once a year the MDAs presents Estimates to cover their needs and requirements which are expected to be prudent, necessary and reasonable, in accordance with the Financial Regulations and Appropriation Act. The Minister presents the Consolidated Revenue and Expenditure Estimates as Appropriation Bill to the Legislature for approval.

2.4. Treasury Control:

This relates to a whole system of controls established in the Executive that ensures the flow of money to the various organizations and their expenditures.

TEL: +233(0)548769918 /+233 (0) 501149296
Facebook Page: www.facebook.com/premiumicaglobal
Website: www.premiumonlinehub.com

2.5. Departmental Control:

This relates to the internal control measures put in place by the MDAs to regulate their activities.

2.6. Financial Control of Local Government Institutions

The financial control of the Local Government Institutions can be appreciated in two realms, namely 'Internal Control' and External control'.

2.6.1.   Internal Controls

The internal control measures are:

- *Issuance of financial authorities; Financial Encumbrance*
- *Appointment of Committees for different services*
- *Centralization of all payments*
- *Preparation of standing orders and instructions on the signing of cheques issued, payments on accounts, etc.*
- *Establishment and maintenance of Internal Audit*
- *Preparation of estimates of income and expenditure for the year.*
- *Budgetary control and feedback processes*

2.6.2.   External Control

The following are the external control measures:

- *Legislative control*
- *Central Government and State Executive Control*
- *Control by the general public comments by individuals on Local Government Institution*
- *External audit control from the Auditor- General*

TEL: +233(0)548769918 /+233 (0) 501149296
Facebook Page: www.facebook.com/premiumicaglobal
Website: www.premiumonlinehub.com

PUBLIC FUND (FUND ACCOUNTING) FINANCIAL ADMINISTRATION ACT, 2003 (ACT 654)

1.1. Introduction

AN ACT to regulate the financial management of the public sector; prescribe the responsibilities of persons entrusted with financial management in the government; ensure the effective and efficient management of state revenue, expenditure, assets, liabilities, resources of the government, the Consolidated Fund and other public funds and to provide for matters related to these.
DATE OF ASSENT: 28th October, 2003.

1.2. PART II—PUBLIC FUNDS

Public funds

5. (1) In accordance with article 175 of the Constitution, the public funds of Ghana consist of the Consolidated Fund, Contingency Fund and such other funds as may be established by or under an Act of Parliament.
(2) Except as otherwise provided in this Act, any fund other than the Consolidated Fund shall be governed by the enactment establishing the fund.

1.2.1. Consolidated Fund:

This is a fund established by law (FAA) into which are paid all revenue and any other monies (receipts and trust monies raised or received on behalf of the government, and from which all lawful disbursements are made on behalf of the government). It was established to serve as a central mechanism for the control of public finances.

- **The Treasury Main Account** is the account opened at Bank of Ghana for the Consolidated Fund. Every fund is expected to have an account with a Bank. The Treasury Main Account is therefore the account for the Consolidated Fund.

6. (1) In accordance with article 176 of the Constitution, there shall be paid into the Consolidated Fund,
(a) revenue or other moneys raised or received for government business or on behalf of the Government; and

(b) any other moneys raised or received in trust for or on behalf of the Government.
  (2) The revenue and other moneys referred to in subsection (1) exclude revenue or other moneys
(a) payable by or under an Act of Parliament into some other fund established for a specific purpose; or
(b) that may, under an Act of Parliament, be retained by the department or agency of Government that received them for the purpose of defraying the expenses of that department or agency.
(3) Where under sub-section (2) provision is made in any enactment for an agency of Government to retain its internally generated funds for the purpose of defraying its expenses pursuant to article 176 (2) (b) of the Constitution, the agency shall make full disclosure of internally generated funds to the Minister at the end of every month.

(4) Notwithstanding any provision to the contrary in any enactment in existence immediately before the coming into force of this Act, no investment in Government securities shall be made of internally generated funds by an agency of Government without prior approval in writing of the Minister.

1.2.1.1. Main Classification / Components of the Consolidated Fund

a. **Below the Line Accounts**: These are subsidiary accounts that relate to all other transactions and balances of the Consolidated Fund-Assets, liabilities and reserves. These accounts do not lapse but continue from year to year.

These accounts do not lapse but continue from year to year

TEL: +233(0)548769918 /+233 (0) 501149296
Facebook Page: www.facebook.com/premiumicaglobal
Website: www.premiumonlinehub.com

b. **Above-the-line-Accounts**

These relates to transactions forming part of the government's annual budget for the provision of goods and services for both recurrent and capital expenditure. These accounts have limited life span that is the lapse at the end of every year.

c. **General Revenue Balance**

The net balance of all the above-the-line-accounts is known as General Revenue Balance. It is made up of unspent revenue where expenditure has not yet been committed. At the end of each financial year this balance is transferred below the line to reserves.

d. **Reserves:**

These are cash balances held by government either in local or foreign banks to meet import bills and other commitments.

1.2.1.2. Reasons for this Classification

(i) Government wants to know its financial position (cash balances) at any point in time, especially weekly, monthly and yearly.

(ii) It also wants to know its total revenue (tax) and other receipts (non-tax) at any particular time. In fact, both the 1992 Constitution and Financial Administration Regulations specify revenues (tax) as separate from other receipts (other monies). Therefore tax (revenue) and other monies (receipts) must be accounted for separately, hence the classifications.

(iii) Government wants to take decisions on expenditure and lending as these activities diminish liquid reserves. Therefore, there is the need to have separate accounts on expenditure and lending. Thus, we have revenue and expenditure accounts (Above-the-line) that relates to transactions forming

TEL: +233(0)548769918 /+233 (0) 501149296
Facebook Page: www.facebook.com/premiumicaglobal
Website: www.premiumonlinehub.com

part of government's recurrent and capital expenditure that have limited lifespan of a year and subsidiary accounts (Below-the-line) that continue from year to year.

(iv)   Government wants to take decisions on borrowing. Government borrowing increases the liquid reserves, making money available for spending, but increases annual expenditure on interest charges. Liquid reserves have to be built to meet redemption of government debts. Decisions on borrowing and investment obviously require separate accounts reflecting cash balances, unspent revenue and uncommitted expenditure.

1.2.1.3. Advances from the Consolidated Fund

22. (1) Subject to Article 181 of the Constitution, no public moneys shall be advanced from the Consolidated Fund except under authority of Regulations made by the Minister and approved by Parliament.

(2) Such Regulations shall specify the terms of release and repayment of advances and require the completion of agreements between the government and the borrowers as a condition for release.
(3) Parliament may require that interest be payable in respect of the advances and shall determine the rate to be paid.

(4) The Controller and Accountant-General may recover an advance or any portion of it that is not repaid or accounted for, as required by Regulations or by agreement out of any moneys payable by the Government to the person to whom the advance was made.

(5) Each accountable advance that is not repaid or accounted for as required by subsection (4) shall be reported in the public accounts.
(6) The Minister shall, when annual estimates are being submitted for the approval of Parliament, include for approval, schedules showing the amounts by which it is proposed that advances shall be increased or diminished in the ensuing financial year and shall seek the prior approval of Parliament for any subsequent revision of the limits set by it.

TEL: +233(0)548769918 /+233 (0) 501149296
Facebook Page: www.facebook.com/premiumicaglobal
Website: www.premiumonlinehub.com

1.2.1.4. Loans from the Consolidated Fund

23. (1) Subject to Article 181 of the Constitution, the President may with the approval of Parliament, authorise the Minister to enter into an agreement to grant a loan from the Consolidated Fund.

(2) An agreement entered into under subsection (1) shall be laid before Parliament and shall not come into operation until it has been approved by Parliament and shall contain a clause to this effect.

(3) Parliament may, by resolution of majority of all the members, authorise the Minister to approve particular classes of loan subject to such limitations as may be specified by Parliament.

(4) The Minister shall, when annual estimates are being submitted for approval by Parliament,

(a) include for approval a schedule of the loans to be payable or repayments to be recovered during the year; and

(b) seek the prior approval of Parliament for any additional amounts that may be required under a general authority to lend, given in accordance with subsection (3).

(5) The amount issued as loans from the Consolidated Fund shall be shown in the public accounts as an asset of the Consolidated Fund until recovery has been effected.

(6) The interest on loans shall be paid into the Consolidated Fund as revenue, and recoveries shall be paid into the Consolidated Fund.
(7) For the purposes of this section the term "loan" means moneys issued from the Consolidated Fund on condition of return or repayment over or after a period of more than one year.

TEL: +233(0)548769918 /+233 (0) 501149296
Facebook Page: www.facebook.com/premiumicaglobal
Website: www.premiumonlinehub.com

1.2.1.5. Equity investments of the Consolidated Fund

24. (1) The President, with the approval of Parliament, may authorise the Minister to provide for, acquire by agreement, or purchase from the Consolidated Fund all or part of the equity capital of a company or other organisation on grounds of state policy.

(2) The Minister shall, when annual estimates are being submitted for approval by Parliament, include for approval a schedule for the equity investments to be made or to be sold or otherwise disposed of during the year.

(3) The amounts issued for provision, acquisition or purchase or equity investments from the Consolidated Fund shall be shown in the public accounts as an asset of the Consolidated Fund until the asset has been sold or otherwise disposed of by authority of Parliament.

(4) The profits and dividends or proceeds of sale arising from the equity investments shall be paid into the Consolidated Fund.

(5) A detailed statement of government's equity investments shall be reported annually in the annual statement of the public accounts.

1.2.1.6. Payment out of the Consolidated Fund

13. (1) A payment shall not be made out of the Consolidated Fund except as provided by article 178 of the Constitution.

(2) A payment shall not be made in excess of the amount granted under an appropriation for any service.

(3) The Minister may by legislative instrument prescribe for the approval of Parliament, procedures to be followed to make payments out of the Consolidated Fund in times of emergency.

TEL: +233(0)548769918 /+233 (0) 501149296
Facebook Page: www.facebook.com/premiumicaglobal
Website: www.premiumonlinehub.com

1.3. SPECIAL FUND

a. Trust funds;
b. Sinking funds;
c. Counterpart funds;
d. Contingency fund;
e. Resolving fund.

1.3.1. Trust funds:

A trust fund is a special fund set up using a donation or bequest from a private person or persons for a public objective and for which the government of Ghana is nominated to act as trustee. That means the government may use the money in accordance with terms of the trust deed, legally belong to the government (FAR 81).

Trust funds allow the government to finance projects without withdrawing monies from the consolidated fund. The fact that the money may be invested means that the government may make full use of the donation.

The acceptance of a trust by the Government shall be sought through the Minister who shall issue the formal acceptance and remit a copy of the Trust Deed to:

- The administering authority;
- The Controller and Accountant – General ; and
- The Auditor – General

1.3.2. Sinking funds:

A sinking fund is a special fund created for the repayment of a loan at some time in the future. It is a fund to set money aside in order to pay for loan and interest as they fall due. Amounts are paid into the sinking fund from the consolidated fund each year are calculated so that they, plus

TEL: +233(0)548769918 /+233 (0) 501149296
Facebook Page: www.facebook.com/premiumicaglobal
Website: www.premiumonlinehub.com

interest earned on them will be sufficient to repay the loan on the due date.

The creation of a sinking fund requires the authorization of the government. When the loan is due for repayment, the Bank of Ghana notifies the Controller and Accountant-General. The money is then transferred to repay the loan. **No other payments may be made from the fund.**

If the amount of the sinking fund is less than the amount needed to repay the loan, the deficit is made up from the consolidated fund. Similarly, if the amount of sinking fund is more than required, the surplus is transferred into the consolidated fund.

1.3.3.   Counterpart funds:

This account/fund takes records of the revenue accrue to the government for the sale of goods from donor countries/partners.

Donors sometimes prefer to finance projects by giving goods rather than cash. In these cases, the government is given the right to sell the goods and use the revenue to finance the specific project.

1.3.4.   The Contingency Fund

The contingency fund is used to help the government cope with disasters and other unexpected events that require public money but have not been specifically included in the budget.

7. (1) In accordance with article 177 of the Constitution, there shall be paid into the Contingency Fund, moneys voted for the purpose by Parliament; and advances may be made from that Fund by the Committee responsible for financial matters in Parliament whenever the Committee is satisfied that there is an urgent or unforeseen need for expenditure for which no other provision exists to meet the need.
(2) Where an advance is made from the Contingency Fund a supplementary estimate shall be presented as soon as possible to Parliament to replace the amount advanced.

TEL: +233(0)548769918 /+233 (0) 501149296
Facebook Page: www.facebook.com/premiumicaglobal
Website: www.premiumonlinehub.com

1.3.5.   Resolving fund:

When the government wants to purchase items and which it plans to resale, the money is paid out of this fund and any revenue accrues is paid into the fund.

1.3.6.   Other special funds

8. (1) Moneys received by or on behalf of the Government for a special purpose and paid into the Consolidated Fund, may be paid out of that Fund subject to the provisions of an Act of Parliament.
(2) Subject to any enactment, interest may be allowed in respect of any money to which subsection (1) applies at rates fixed by the Minister in Regulations or administratively.

1.3.6.1. Custody of public moneys and moneys received in trust for Government

9. (1) A person who collects or receives public moneys or moneys in trust for Government shall keep a record of receipts and deposits in a form and manner that the Controller and Accountant-General may prescribe.

(2) Any person who collects or receives any public moneys or moneys in trust for Government without the prior authority of the Controller and Accountant-General shall immediately pay the moneys into the Consolidated Fund and explain to the Controller and Accountant-General the circumstances under which these moneys came into the possession of that person.

(3) Persons authorised to collect or receive public moneys and moneys in trust for Government shall pay the moneys promptly into the Consolidated Fund in such manner as may be prescribed in regulations or as the Controller and Accountant-General may direct.

TEL: +233(0)548769918 /+233 (0) 501149296
Facebook Page: www.facebook.com/premiumicaglobal
Website: www.premiumonlinehub.com

1.3.6.2. Payment for services rendered by Government departments

2. Where a service is rendered by a department to any person and the Minister is of the opinion that a charge for that service should be borne by the person to whom the service is rendered, the Minister may subject to the provisions of an enactment relating to that service, prescribe the fees to be charged.

1.3.6.3. Receipt and payment of deposits

11. (1) Where money is received by a public officer from any person, such as a deposit to ensure the doing of an act or thing, the public officer shall hold or dispose of the money in such manner as the Minister may prescribe.

(2) Where money is paid by a person to a public officer for a purpose that is not fulfilled, the money may, less such sum as in the opinion of the Minister is properly attributed to service rendered, be returned or repaid or otherwise dealt with as the Minister may direct.

(3) Money paid to the credit of the Consolidated Fund, not being public money, may be returned or repaid in such manner as the Minister may prescribe.

(4) The Minister may determine the amount of cash or securities held to meet obligations under this section

TEL: +233(0)548769918 /+233 (0) 501149296
Facebook Page: www.facebook.com/premiumicaglobal
Website: www.premiumonlinehub.com

1.3.6.4. Deletion from the accounts

12. (1) The Minister may, subject to the approval of Parliament, in the public interest, recommend the deletion from the public accounts or other government accounts, in whole or in part, of any obligation or debt due to the Government or any claim by the Government.

(2) The deletion from the accounts does not constitute a remission of the obligation, debt or claim and does not debar subsequent proceedings for recovery, should the Minister see fit.

(3) The Minister may by regulation delegate the power of deletion under this section, subject to such terms and conditions as the Minister may require, to any public officer who shall personally exercise the delegated powers.

(4) The obligations, debts and claims deleted from the accounts shall be reported in financial statements required under sections 54 and 55 of this Act.

1.4. Legal Provisions

1.4.1.   Disbursement of Special Funds

All disbursements out of a Special Fund shall be made by authorization of the administering authority of the Special Fund, quoting the rules governing the operation of the Fund and any rule pertaining to the particular transaction.

1.4.2.   Accounting for Special Fund

A head of department responsible for the administering a Special Fund shall keep accounts of all transaction in accordance with procedures laid in Department Accounting Instructions.

TEL: +233(0)548769918 /+233 (0) 501149296
Facebook Page: www.facebook.com/premiumicaglobal
Website: www.premiumonlinehub.com

1.4.3. Annual account of Special Funds

- A head of department responsible for administering a Special Fund shall prepare an annual report and financial statements of transactions in relation to the Special Fund, which shall be separately certified by the Auditor- General

- Unless the rules relating to the Special Fund require a separate publication, the annual reports and financial statements of the Fund shall be included in the departmental annual statement of account prepared in accordance with section 41 of the Financial Administration Act, 2003, (Act 654).

1.5. The District Assembly Common Fund (DAFC)
1.5.1. Introduction

The Common Fund under Act 455 of 1993 is defined as "a fund consisting of all monies allocated by parliament and any interest and dividends accruing from investments of monies from the common fund".

1.5.2. Functions of the District Assembly Common Fund Administrator

- Propose a formula annually for the distribution of the common fund for approval by parliament.

- To administer and distribute monies paid into the common fund among the district Assemblies in accordance with the formula approved by Parliament.

- To report in writing to the minister of Finance on how allocations made from the funds have been utilized by the District Assemblies.

- To perform any other functions that may be directed by the President

TEL: +233(0)548769918 /+233 (0) 501149296
Facebook Page: www.facebook.com/premiumicaglobal
Website: www.premiumonlinehub.com

1.5.3. Challenges facing the District Assembly Common Fund administration

- Lack of transparency in determining what goes into the DACF

- Since the inception of the DACF, the Minister of Local Government has not issued guidelines to MMDAs on the utilization of the land.
- The constitution obligation on Parliament to make provisions for the allocation of not less than 5% of total revenues of Ghana into the DACF seems unfulfilled.

- The DACF has encountered what is called "statutory deduction" from the fund yearly. These deductions are used to fund bulk purchases and other programmes of Central Government.
- A portion of the DACF is used to fund some activities of the Regional Coordinating Councils who do not qualify under the constitution.

- After approval of budget by District Assemblies, the ministry authorizes deductions from their DACF allocations without notification whatsoever, thereby seriously undermining the development programmes of the MMDAs
- Delays in the release of the DACF to the districts on time for the necessary developmental projects to be carried out.
- Misuse of the part of the allocation to the MPs for political gains instead of developmental projects.

1.5.4. Ministerial directives for fund utilization

The Finance Minister is expected to consult with the minister of Local Government and Rural Development to define the areas in which the common fund can be used for development from period, to period and circulate this policy guideline to the various parties involved in the disbursement process.

TEL: +233(0)548769918 /+233 (0) 501149296
Facebook Page: www.facebook.com/premiumicaglobal
Website: www.premiumonlinehub.com

1.6. The Road Fund

An Act of Parliament (Act 536) established the Fund on 29th August, 1997.

1.6.1. Objectives/ Purpose of the Road Fund

The purposes of the Road Fund include:

(a) To finance routine, period maintenance and rehabilitation of public roads in the country.

(b) To assist the Metropolitan, Municipal and district Assemblies in the exercise of their functions relevant to public roads under the Act.

1.6.2. Sources of Monies to the Fund:

(a) Government levy on Petrol, diesel and refined fuel.

(b) Bridges, ferry and road tolls collected by the authorities.

(c) Vehicle licence and inspection fees

(d) International transit fees collected from foreign vehicles entering the country.

(e) Such moneys as the Minister for Finance in consultation with the Minister for Roads may determine

1.6.3. Charges to the Fund
- Routine and periodic maintenance of road and related facilities;
- Upgrading and rehabilitation of roads
- Road safety activities
- Selected road safety activities; and
- Such other relevant matters as may be determined by the Board.

TEL: +233(0)548769918 /+233 (0) 501149296
Facebook Page: www.facebook.com/premiumicaglobal
Website: www.premiumonlinehub.com

1.7. Ghana Education Trust Fund (GETFund)

1.7.1. Introduction

The GETfund was established by an Act of Parliament (Act 581) on 25th August 2000 to assist nation-wide with financing of education; to provide for the management of the funds and financing for related matters.

1.7.2. Objective of the fund

To provide finance to supplement the provision of education at all levels by the government.

1.7.3. Mode of disbursement

Disbursement of monies is made through the Ministry of Education (MoE) and National Council of Treasury Education (NCTE), the Scholarship Secretariat and the Social Security and National Insurance Trust (SSNIT).

1.7.4. Who benefits from the Fund?

Public educational institutes, Basic schools, 2nd cycle schools and tertiary institutions in Ghana.

1.7.5 Areas of Benefit
- Essential academic facilities and infrastructure

- Gifted but needy student as a grant of scholarship to study in Ghana, through a supplementary funding to the Scholarship Secretariat
- Loans schemes mechanisms for students in accredited tertiary institutions in Ghana
- Training of brilliant students as members of faculties and researchers.

- Educational activities and programmes of relevance to the nation.

TEL: +233(0)548769918 /+233 (0) 501149296
Facebook Page: www.facebook.com/premiumicaglobal
Website: www.premiumonlinehub.com

1.8. PETROLEUM REVENUE FUNDS:

1.8.1. Introduction

Petroleum Revenue Management Act 815 was enacted in 2011 to provide the framework for the collection, allocation and management of petroleum revenue in a responsible, transparent and accountable manner for the benefit of the citizens of Ghana.

1.8.2. Sources of petroleum revenue include:

- Royalties on oil and gas exploration.

- Direct or indirect revenues accruing to government from involvement in the exploration business. That is, proceed from sales of government share of crude oil.

- Income taxes and other fees received from upstream and midstream companies.

- Income taxes from national oil company.

- Dividend and other benefits from national oil company.

- Any other revenues relating to oil and gas industry.

1.8.3. Types of funds under the Petroleum Revenue Management Act 2011 (Act 815)

1.8.3.1. Petroleum Holding Fund

It is a fund established to receive and disburse petroleum revenues due to the state. All petroleum revenues are required to be deposited into the petroleum holding fund with Bank of Ghana for subsequent transfer to

TEL: +233(0)548769918 /+233 (0) 501149296
Facebook Page: www.facebook.com/premiumicaglobal
Website: www.premiumonlinehub.com

the stabilization fund, heritage fund and the consolidated fund. The fund can neither be used to provide credit to government nor used as collateral for debt, guarantees, commitments or their liabilities.

1.8.3.2. Ghana Stabilization Fund

It is a fund established to cushion the impact or sustain public expenditure capacity during period of unanticipated petroleum revenue shortfall. An approved percentage is transferred from the petroleum holding fund to this fund.

1.8.3.3. Ghana Heritage Fund

It is created to provide an endowment to support the development for the future generations when the petroleum resources have been depleted. Any excess petroleum revenues in a particular year are payable into this fund. In addition, an approved percentage is transferred from the petroleum holding fund to this fund.

1.9. VIREMENT

1.9.1.   Introduction

Virement is the application, under the specific authority of the MoFEP in each case, of savings on one or more subheads to meet excess expenditure on another subhead or subheads in the same Vote, including any new subheads opened during the course of the year.

Virement can only be made by seeking approval from the MoFEP.

1.9.2.   *Authority for Virement*

Parliament is the authority to grant any request for such funds switching after a spending organization makes an application. The authority can also be given by the Finance Minister. However, the Minister may delegate the power to authorize virements to a head of department, stating clearly the terms and extent of such delegation.

TEL: +233(0)548769918 /+233 (0) 501149296
Facebook Page: www.facebook.com/premiumicaglobal
Website: www.premiumonlinehub.com

1.9.3. Features for or conditions for Virment

The following are the conditions for virement:

- *Virement is not allowed between line items of expenditure. That's it is not possible to switch between votes; it is possible between sub-items of expenditure.*
- *It is allowed where savings have been made in other expenditure sub items.*
- *It is allowed where the savings do not arise from the deferment of expenditure;*
- *It is allowed if the extra funds are required for existing services, but not for any new services;*
- *It is not allowed for capital expenditure, or expenditure which can lead to incurring extra expenditure in the future;*
- *It is not allowed for an expenditure that will end up in a change in government policy.*
- *It is not allowed for compensation of employees.*

2.0. Conditions for payment by MDAs

Payment shall only be made for work done, goods supplied or services rendered unless the head of MDA certifies that:

- *The work has been performed, the goods supplied or the service rendered, and that the price charged is according to the contract.*

- *Where payment is to be made before the completion of the work, delivery of goods or rendering of the service, which the payment is in accordance with the contract.*

- *Where taxes are required to be paid in respect of payment of work done, whether under the contract or not, the head of department concerned shall be responsible to ensure that any tax is paid.*

TEL: +233(0)548769918 /+233 (0) 501149296
Facebook Page: www.facebook.com/premiumicaglobal
Website: www.premiumonlinehub.com

- *It is the duty of any officer conducting financial business to bring to the notice of the appropriate authority any case where application of the law of financial instructions leads to results that may be contrary to public interest.*

- *The accounting officers have specific responsibilities*

- *A head of department of a MDA shall issue departmental accounting instructions to regulate the financial business of the department indicating the duties to be performed by specified officers, the accounts to be kept and returns submitted, and such other instructions as may be required for the proper conduct of such business.*

2.1. APPROPRIATIONS:
2.1.1. Introduction

An Appropriation is a budgetary tool used in governmental accounting to control spending. It can also be referred to as an allocation, or set aside of monies for specific purposes.

An Appropriation Bill covers the combined Estimates of the spending organizations and this Bill is passed into Appropriation Act after all the Estimates have been examined and debated upon.

2.1.2. *Functions of an Appropriation Act*
a. *The Appropriation Act Authorizes the estimates of the organizations;*
b. *It gives agreement to the Ambit (an area in which something acts or operates or has power or control) of the Vote*
c. *It serves as a reference point for any misunderstanding and disagreements*
d. *It denotes by implication ultra- vires acts of any organization.*

TEL: +233(0)548769918 /+233 (0) 501149296
Facebook Page: www.facebook.com/premiumicaglobal
Website: www.premiumonlinehub.com

2.1.3. *Appropriation – in – Aid*

This refers to any income that a department receives outside the consolidated fund. This income is expected to be deducted from the total supply estimates or appropriations needed by the organization hence this reduces the amount to be paid out of the Consolidated Fund.

Appropriation – in Aid may include the following:

- *Charges for services;*

- *Pension contributions;*

- *Rentals and proceeds from certain sales*

- *With the prior agreement of the MoFEP, the proceeds from the sale of assets for the funding of high priority capital programmes or project;*

- *Fines, forfeiture or cost recovered.*

TEL: +233(0)548769918 /+233 (0) 501149296
Facebook Page: www.facebook.com/premiumicaglobal
Website: www.premiumonlinehub.com

2.2. Accounting Entries for Common Transactions at the Ministerial Level

1	Budgetary Grants due from Parliament Approval		
	DR	Consolidated Fund	With the approved budgetary grant
	CR	Budgetary Grant Account	
	This is like the income for the Department		
2	Grants transferred to the CAGD's to be held in trust for the Department or Ministry		
	DR	Accountant General's Department	
	CR	Consolidated Fund	
3	Grants received directly from the Consolidated Fund		
	DR	Bank/ Cash Account/ Imprest Account	
	CR	Consolidated Fund	
4	Payments made by the CAGD on behalf of the Department or Ministry		
	DR	Expenditure Account (All Expenditures)	

TEL: +233(0)548769918 /+233 (0) 501149296
Facebook Page: www.facebook.com/premiumicaglobal
Website: www.premiumonlinehub.com

	CR	CAGD	
5		Payment made by the particular department or Ministry for administration expenses and for services	
	DR	Expenditure Account (Goods and Services)	
	CR	Bank/ Cash Account	
6		Income generated by the Department that is maintained is referred to as appropriation- in- aid	
	DR	Bank (with total proceeds received)	
	CR	Appropriation in – aid (with part of the income maintained as finance)	
	CR	Consolidated Fund Account(with income returned to government)	
7		When income generated by the unit is returned to central government, that is, if all Appropriation-in-Aid is returned to government then	
	DR	Bank Account	

TEL: +233(0)548769918 /+233 (0) 501149296
Facebook Page: www.facebook.com/premiumicaglobal
Website: www.premiumonlinehub.com

	CR	Consolidated Fund Account	
	With the total amount of the appropriation-in-aid		
8	At the end of the accounting year		
	a	Close all expense accounts by transfer to the parliamentary grant account to obtain the amount on the parliamentary grant account as under/over spent for the period;	
	b	Prepare the appropriation account in summary form, showing comparison with budgetary estimates and covering all sub-heads of the budget.	

TEL: +233(0)548769918 /+233 (0) 501149296
Facebook Page: www.facebook.com/premiumicaglobal
Website: www.premiumonlinehub.com

PUBLIC PROCUREMENT: THE PUBLIC PROCUREMENT ACT

1.1. Introduction THE PUBLIC PROCUREMENT ACT, 2003

AN ACT to provide for public procurement, establish the Public Procurement Board; make administrative and institutional arrangements for procurement; stipulate tendering procedures and provide for purposes connected with these.
DATE OF ASSENT: 31st December, 2003

1.2. PART I—ESTABLISHMENT OF THE PUBLIC PROCUREMENT BOARD

1.2.1. Public Procurement Board

(1) There is established by this Act a body to be known as the Public Procurement Board, referred to in this Act as "the Board".

(2) The Board shall be a body corporate with perpetual succession and a common seal and may sue and be sued in its corporate name.

(3) The Board may acquire, hold, manage or dispose of any movable or immovable property in connection with the discharge of its functions and may enter into contracts and transactions that are reasonably related to its functions.

1.2.2. GOVERNING STRUCTURE OF THE PROCUREMENT BOARD.

1.2.3. Object of the Board

2. The object of the Board is to harmonise the processes of public procurement in the public service to secure a judicious, economic and efficient use of state resources in public procurement and ensure that public procurement is carried out in a fair, transparent and non-discriminatory manner.

TEL: +233(0)548769918 /+233 (0) 501149296
Facebook Page: www.facebook.com/premiumicaglobal
Website: www.premiumonlinehub.com

2.1.1. Functions of the Board

3. In furtherance of its object the Board shall perform the following functions:

- (a) make proposals for the formulation of policies on procurement;

- (b) ensure policy implementation and human resource development for public procurement;

- (c) develop draft rules, instructions, other regulatory documentation on public procurement and formats for public procurement documentation;

- (d) monitor and supervise public procurement and ensure compliance with statutory requirements;

- (e) have the right to obtain information concerning public procurement from contracting authorities;

- (f) establish and implement an information system relating to public procurement;

- (g) publish a monthly Public Procurement Bulletin which shall contain information germane to public procurement, including proposed procurement notices, notices of invitation to tender and contract award information;

- (h) assess the operations of the public procurement processes and submit proposals for improvement of the processes;

- (i) present annual reports to the Minister on the public procurement processes;

TEL: +233(0)548769918 /+233 (0) 501149296
Facebook Page: www.facebook.com/premiumicaglobal
Website: www.premiumonlinehub.com

(j)   facilitate the training of public officials involved in public procurement at various levels;

(k)   develop, promote and support training and professional development of persons engaged in public procurement, and ensure adherence by the trained persons to ethical standards;

(l)   advise Government on issues relating to public procurement;

(m) organise and participate in the administrative review procedures in Part VII of this Act;

(n)   plan and co-ordinate technical assistance in the field of public procurement;

(o)   maintain a register of procurement entities and members of and secretaries to tender committees of public procurement entities;

(p)   maintain a data base of suppliers, contractors and consultants and a record of prices to assist in the work of procurement entities;

(q)   investigate and debar from procurement practice under this Act, suppliers, contractors and consultants who have seriously neglected their obligations under a public procurement contract, have provided false information about their qualifications, or offered inducements of the kind referred to in section 32 of this Act;

(r)   maintain a list of firms that have been debarred from participating in public procurement and communicate the list to procurement entities on a regular basis;

TEL: +233(0)548769918 /+233 (0) 501149296
Facebook Page: www.facebook.com/premiumicaglobal
Website: www.premiumonlinehub.com

(s) hold an annual forum for consultations on public procurement and other related issues;

(t) assist the local business community to become competitive and efficient suppliers to the public sector; and

(u) perform such other functions as are incidental to the attainment of the objects of this Act.

2.1.2. Membership of the Board

4. (1) The Board comprises

(a) a chairperson, who shall be a person competent and experienced in public procurement;

(b) a vice-chairperson, who shall be elected by members from among their number;

(c) four persons from the public sector made up of a representative of the Attorney General and three other persons, nominated by the Minister, one of whom is a woman and each of whom shall have experience in public procurement and be familiar with governmental and multi-lateral agency procurement procedures;

(d) three persons from the private sector who have experience in procurement at least one of whom is a woman;

(e) the Chief Executive of the Board.

(2) The members of the Board shall be appointed by the President acting in consultation with the Council of State.

TEL: +233(0)548769918 /+233 (0) 501149296
Facebook Page: www.facebook.com/premiumicaglobal
Website: www.premiumonlinehub.com

2.1.3. Term of office

5. (1) A member of the Board other than the Chief Executive,

(a) shall hold office for a term of four years and is eligible for re-appointment for another term only;

(b) may in writing addressed to the President through the Minister resign from office.

(2) A member may be removed from office by the President acting in consultation with the Council of State for inability to perform the functions of office, infirmity or any sufficient cause.

(3) Members shall be paid allowances determined by the Minister.

2.1.4. Meetings of the Board

6. (1) The Board shall meet for the despatch of business at such times and places as the
Chairperson may determine but shall meet at least once every three months.

(2) The Chairperson shall preside at meetings of the Board and in the absence of the
Chairperson the Vice-Chairperson shall preside and in the absence of both, the members shall elect one of their number to preside.

(3) The quorum for a meeting of the Board shall be five including the Chief Executive.

(4) The Board may co-opt any person to act as adviser at a meeting of the Board, except that a co-opted person does not have the right to vote on any matter before the Board for decision.

(5) The validity of the proceedings of the Board shall not be affected by a vacancy among its members or by a defect in the appointment or qualification of a member.

TEL: +233(0)548769918 /+233 (0) 501149296
Facebook Page: www.facebook.com/premiumicaglobal
Website: www.premiumonlinehub.com

(6) Except as otherwise expressly provided, the Board shall determine the procedure for its meetings.

2.1.5. Committees of the Board

7. The Board may for the discharge of its functions appoint committees of the Board comprising members of the Board or non-members or both and may assign to them such functions as the Board may determine except that a committee composed entirely of non-members may only advise the Board.

2.1.6. Secretariat of the Board

8. (1) The Board shall have a Secretariat with such divisions and structures determined by the Board as may be necessary for the effective execution of its functions.

(2) The Board shall have an officer to be designated the Secretary who shall perform the function of keeping accurate records of proceedings and decisions of the Board and such other functions as the Chief Executive may direct.

(3) The Board may engage such consultants and advisers as it may require for the proper and efficient discharge of the functions of the Secretariat.

2.1.7. Chief Executive of the Board

9. (1) The Chief Executive of the Board shall be appointed in accordance with article 195 of the Constitution.

(2) The Chief Executive shall hold office on such terms and conditions as may be in the letter of appointment to office.

(3) Subject to such general directions as the Board may give, the Chief Executive is responsible for the day-to-day administration of the Secretariat of the Board and the implementation of the decisions of the Board.

TEL: +233(0)548769918 /+233 (0) 501149296
Facebook Page: www.facebook.com/premiumicaglobal
Website: www.premiumonlinehub.com

(4) The Chief Executive may delegate functions of the office as Chief Executive to any officer of the Secretariat but shall not be relieved of the ultimate responsibility for the discharge of the delegated function.

2.1.8. Expenses of the Board

10. Parliament shall provide the Board with such monies as it may require meeting its expenditure. The Board may also receive monies from other sources approved by the Minister.

2.1.9. Accounts and audit

11. (1) The Board shall keep books of account and proper records in relation to them and the accounts books and records of the Board shall be in a form prescribed by the Controller and Accountant-General and approved by the Auditor-General.
(2) The books and accounts of the Board shall be audited annually by the Auditor- General or by an auditor appointed by the Auditor-General.

2.1.10. Financial year of Board

12. The financial year of the Board shall be the same as the financial year of the Government.

2.1.11. Annual report

13. (1) The Board shall within three months after the end of each year, submit to the Minister a written report indicating the activities and operations of the Board in respect of the preceding year.

(2) The annual report shall include a copy of the audited accounts together with the Auditor General's report and the Minister shall as soon as practicable after receipt of the annual report submit the report to Parliament with such comment as the Minister considers necessary.

TEL: +233(0)548769918 /+233 (0) 501149296
Facebook Page: www.facebook.com/premiumicaglobal
Website: www.premiumonlinehub.com

2.2. PROCUREMENT STRUCTURES IN THE PUBLIC PROCUREMENT ACT.

PART II—PROCUREMENT STRUCTURES

2.2.1. Scope of application

14. (1) This Act applies to

(a) the procurement of goods, works and services, financed in whole or in part from public funds except where the Minister decides that it is in the national interest to use a different procedure;

(b) functions that pertain to procurement of goods, works and services including the description of requirements and invitation of sources, preparation, selection and award of contract and the phases of contract administration;

(c) the disposal of public stores and equipment; and

(d) procurement with funds or loans taken or guaranteed by the State and foreign aid funds except where the applicable loan agreement, guarantee contract or foreign agreement provides the procedure for the use of the funds.

(2) Without limiting subsection (1), this Act applies to

(a) central management agencies;

(b) government ministries, departments and agencies;

(c) subvented agencies;

(d) governance institutions;
(e) state owned enterprises to the extent that they utilise public funds;

(f) public universities, public schools, colleges and hospitals;

TEL: +233(0)548769918 /+233 (0) 501149296
Facebook Page: www.facebook.com/premiumicaglobal
Website: www.premiumonlinehub.com

(g) the Bank of Ghana and financial institutions such as public trusts, pension funds, insurance companies and building societies which are wholly owned by the State or in which the State has majority interest;

(h) institutions established by Government for the general welfare of the public or community.

(3) Where the Minister decides under subsection (1)(a) that it is in the national interest to use a different procedure, the Minister shall define and publish in the Gazette the method of procurement to be followed in order to serve the interest of economy.

2.2.2.   Procurement entity

15. (1) A procurement entity is responsible for procurement, subject to this Act and to such other conditions as may be laid down in the procurement regulations and administrative instructions of the Minister, issued in consultation with the Board.

(2) The head of an entity and any officer to whom responsibility is delegated are responsible and accountable for action taken and for any instructions with regard to the implementation of this Act that may be issued by the Minister acting in consultation with the Board.

(3) Procurement decisions of an entity shall be taken in a corporate manner and any internal units concerned shall contribute to the decision making process.

(4) The head of an entity is responsible to ensure that provisions of this Act are complied with; and concurrent approval by any Tender Review Board shall not absolve the head of entity from accountability for a contract that may be determined to have been procured in a manner that is inconsistent with the provisions of this Act.

TEL: +233(0)548769918 /+233 (0) 501149296
Facebook Page: www.facebook.com/premiumicaglobal
Website: www.premiumonlinehub.com

2.2.2.1. Declaration of procurement entity

16. (1) The Minister may, in consultation with the Board, by notice in the Gazette, declare any entity or person to be a procurement entity.

(2) Subject to approval by the Board, a procurement entity may undertake procurement in accordance with established private sector or commercial practices if

(a) the procurement entity is legally and financially autonomous and operates under commercial law;
(b) it is beyond contention that public sector procurement procedures are not suitable, considering the strategic nature of the procurement; and

(c) the proposed procurement method will ensure value for money, provide competition and transparency to the extent possible.

2.2.3.   Tender Committee

17. (1) Each procurement entity shall establish a Tender Committee in the manner set out in Schedule 1.

(2) In the performance of its functions, a Tender Committee shall

(a) ensure that at every stage of the procurement activity, procedures prescribed in this Act have been followed;

(b) exercise sound judgment in making procurement decisions; and

(c) refer to the appropriate Tender Review Board for approval, any procurement above its approval threshold, taking into consideration the fact that approval above the Entity Committee is a one stop only approval.

2.2.3.1. Meetings of Tender Committee

18. The Tender Committee shall meet at least once every quarter and notice of the meetings shall be given at least two weeks prior to the scheduled date of the meeting.

TEL: +233(0)548769918 /+233 (0) 501149296
Facebook Page: www.facebook.com/premiumicaglobal
Website: www.premiumonlinehub.com

2.2.4. Tender evaluation panel

19. (1) Each procurement entity shall appoint a tender evaluation panel with the required expertise to evaluate tenders and assist the Tender Committee in its work.

(2) In the performance of its functions, a tender evaluation panel shall proceed according to the predetermined and published evaluation criteria.

2.2.5. Tender Review Boards

20. (1) There shall be established at each level of public procurement the following
Tender Review Boards in the manner set out in Schedule 2

(a) Central Tender Review Board;
(b) Ministerial/Headquarters Tender Review Boards;
(c) Regional Tender Review Boards;
(d) District Tender Review Boards.

(2) A Tender Review Board shall perform the following functions:

(a) in relation to the particular procurement under consideration, review the activities at each step of the procurement cycle leading to the selection of the lowest evaluated bid, best offer, by the procurement entity in order to ensure compliance with the provisions of this Act and its operating instructions and guidelines;

(b) subject to subsection (2) (a), give concurrent approval or otherwise to enable the procurement entity continue with the procurement process;

(c) furnish the Board with reports in a prescribed format;

(d) participate in public procurement forum; and

(e) review decisions of heads of entities in respect of a complaint.

TEL: +233(0)548769918 /+233 (0) 501149296
Facebook Page: www.facebook.com/premiumicaglobal
Website: www.premiumonlinehub.com

(3) A Tender Review Board may engage the services of such consultants and advisers, or co-opt persons with specialized expertise as it may require for the proper and efficient discharge of its functions.

1.4. PART III—PROCUREMENT RULES

1.4.1. Procurement plan

21. (1) A procurement entity shall prepare a procurement plan to support its approved programme and the plan shall indicate

(a) contract packages,

(b) estimated cost for each package,

(c) the procurement method, and

(d) processing steps and times.

(2) A procurement entity shall submit to its Tender Committee not later than one month to the end of the financial year the procurement plan for the following year for approval.

(3) After budget approval and at quarterly intervals after that, each procurement entity shall submit an update of the procurement plan to the Tender Committee.

(4) The procurement entity shall send to the Tender Review Board, procurement notices for contracts and procurement plans above the thresholds stipulated in Schedule 3 for publication in the Public Procurement Bulletin.

(5) A procurement entity shall not divide a procurement order into parts or lower the value of a procurement order to avoid the application of the procedures for public procurement in this Act.

TEL: +233(0)548769918 /+233 (0) 501149296
Facebook Page: www.facebook.com/premiumicaglobal
Website: www.premiumonlinehub.com

1.4.2. Qualification of tenderers

22. (1) A tenderer in public procurement shall

(a) possess the necessary

(i) professional and technical qualifications and competence;

(ii) financial resources;

(iii) equipment and other physical facilities;

(iv) managerial capability, reliability, experience in the procurement object and reputation; and

(v) the personnel to perform the procurement contract;

(b) have the legal capacity to enter the contract;

(c) be solvent, not be in receivership, bankrupt or in the process of being wound up, not have its business activities suspended and not be the subject of legal proceedings that would materially affect its capacity to enter into a contract;

(d) have fulfilled its obligations to pay taxes and social security contributions and any paid compensation due for damage caused to property by pollution;

(e) have directors or officers who have not in any country been

(i) convicted of any criminal offence relating to their professional conduct or to making false statements or misrepresentations as to their qualifications to enter into a procurement contract, within a period of ten years preceding the commencement of the procurement proceedings; or

(ii) disqualified pursuant to administrative suspension or disbarment proceedings.

TEL: +233(0)548769918 /+233 (0) 501149296
Facebook Page: www.facebook.com/premiumicaglobal
Website: www.premiumonlinehub.com

(f) meet such other criteria as the procurement entity considers appropriate.

(2) The procurement entity may require tenderers to provide appropriate documentary evidence or other information that it considers useful to satisfy itself that the tenderers are qualified in accordance with the criteria referred to in subsection (1).

(3) Any requirement established pursuant to this section stated in the tender documents or other documents for invitation of proposals shall apply equally to the tenderers.

(4) The procurement entity shall evaluate the qualifications of candidates in accordance with the criteria and procedures stated in the documents referred to in subsection (3).

(5) The procurement entity shall disqualify a tenderer who submits a document containing false information for purposes of qualification.

(6) The procurement entity may disqualify a candidate if it finds at any time that the information submitted concerning the qualifications of the candidate was materially inaccurate or materially incomplete.

1.4.3.   Prequalification proceedings

23. (1) A procurement entity may engage in prequalification proceedings to identify tenderers who are qualified prior to the submission of tenders.

(2) Tenderers for prequalification proceedings shall meet the qualification criteria of the procurement entity and the proceedings shall be conducted pursuant to Part IV and V.

(3) A procurement entity shall supply a set of prequalification documents to each supplier or contractor that requests them; and the price that a procurement entity charges for the prequalification documents shall reflect the cost of printing and provision to suppliers or contractors.

(4) The prequalification documents shall include

TEL: +233(0)548769918 /+233 (0) 501149296
Facebook Page: www.facebook.com/premiumicaglobal
Website: www.premiumonlinehub.com

(a) Instructions to prepare and submit prequalification applications;

(b) a summary of the main terms and conditions required for the procurement contract to be entered into as a result of the procurement proceedings;

(c) any documentary evidence or other information that must be submitted by suppliers or contractors to demonstrate their qualifications;

(d) the manner and place for the submission of applications to prequalify and the deadline for the submission, expressed as a specific date and time which allows sufficient time for suppliers or contractors to prepare and submit their applications, taking into account the reasonable needs of the procurement entity;

(e) any other requirement that may be established by the procurement entity in conformity with this Act and procurement regulations relating to the preparation and submission of applications to prequalify and to the prequalification proceedings; and

(f) in proceedings under Part V, the information required to be specified in the invitation to tender by section 48(1)(a) to (e) and if the information required under section 48(1) (a) to (e) is already known, the information required under paragraphs (j) and (k) of section 48(1).

(5) The procurement entity shall respond to any request by a supplier or contractor for clarification of the prequalification documents if the request is made at least within ten days prior to the deadline for the submission of applications to prequalify.

(6) The response by the procurement entity shall be given within a reasonable time and in any event within a period of at least seven working days so as to enable the supplier or contractor to make a timely submission of its application to prequalify.

(7) The response to any request that might reasonably be expected to be of interest to other suppliers or contractors shall, without identifying the

TEL: +233(0)548769918 /+233 (0) 501149296
Facebook Page: www.facebook.com/premiumicaglobal
Website: www.premiumonlinehub.com

source of the request, be communicated to other suppliers or contractors provided with the prequalification documents by the procurement entity.

1.4.4. Rejection of tenders, proposals and quotations

29. (1) A procurement entity may reject tenders, proposals and quotations at any time prior to acceptance if the grounds for the rejection are specified in the tender documents or in the request for proposals or quotations.

(2) The grounds for rejection shall be communicated to the tenderer but justification for the rejection is not required and the procurement entity shall not incur liability towards the tenderer.

(3) Notice of the rejection shall be given to participating tenderers within two days from the date the procurement entity decides to discontinue with the tender process.

(4) If the decision to reject tenders is taken before the closing date, tenders received shall be returned unopened to the tenderers submitting them.

(5) The rejection of the tender, proposal, offer or quotation with reasons shall be recorded in the procurement proceedings and promptly communicated to the supplier or contractor.

1.4.5. Entry into force of the procurement contract

30. (1) In tender proceedings, acceptance of the tender and entry into force of the procurement contract shall be carried out in accordance with section 65 of this Act.
(2) In the other methods of procurement, the manner of entry into force of the procurement contract shall be notified to the suppliers or contractors at the time those proposals, offers or quotations are requested

TEL: +233(0)548769918 /+233 (0) 501149296
Facebook Page: www.facebook.com/premiumicaglobal
Website: www.premiumonlinehub.com

1.4.5. Public notice of procurement contract awards

31. (1) A procurement entity shall promptly publish notice of procurement contract awards.

(2) Regulations shall provide for the manner of publication of the notice of procurement contract awards.

1.4.6.   Inducements from suppliers, contractors and consultants

32. A procurement entity shall reject a tender, proposal, offer or quotation if the supplier, contractor or consultant that submitted it offers, gives or agrees to give, directly or indirectly, to any current or former officer or employee of the procurement entity or other governmental authority,

(a) a gratuity in any form;

(b) an offer of employment; or

(c) any other thing of service or value as an inducement with respect to anything connected with a procurement entity and procurement proceedings.

1.4.7.   Description of goods, works or services
33. (1) Any

(a) specifications, plans, drawings and designs that provide the technical or quality characteristics of goods, works, or services to be procured;

(b) requirements on testing and test methods, packaging, marketing, labelling or conformity certifications; and

(c) symbols and terminology description of services that create obstacles to participation including obstacles based on nationality tenderers shall not be included or used in prequalification documents, invitation documents or other documents for invitation of proposals, offers or quotations.

TEL: +233(0)548769918 /+233 (0) 501149296
Facebook Page: www.facebook.com/premiumicaglobal
Website: www.premiumonlinehub.com

(2) The provisions in subsection (1) shall be based on objective technical and quality characteristics of the goods, works or services to be procured and there shall be no requirement of or reference to a particular trade mark, name, patent, design, type, specific origin or producer, unless a precise or intelligible way of describing the characteristics of the goods, works or services to be procured does not exist, in which case, the words "or equivalent" shall be included.

(3) Standardised features, requirements, symbols and terminology relating to the technical and quality characteristics of the goods, works or services to be procured shall be used, where available, to formulate any specifications, plans, drawings and designs to be included in the prequalification documents, invitation documents or other documents for invitation of proposals, offers or quotations.

1.5. PART IV—METHODS OF PROCUREMENT

1.5.1. Competitive tendering

35. (1) A procurement entity shall procure goods, services or works by competitive tendering except as provided in this Part.

(2) A procurement entity shall use the quality and cost-based method of selection in Part VI when selecting consultants unless the procurement entity determines that

(a) it is feasible to formulate detailed specifications and tendering proceedings or other methods of procurement which are more appropriate taking into account the nature of the services to be procured; or

(b) it is more appropriate to use a method of selection referred to in Part VI if the conditions for the use of that method are satisfied.

(3) If the procurement entity uses the method of procurement other than competitive tendering, it shall include in the record required a statement

TEL: +233(0)548769918 /+233 (0) 501149296
Facebook Page: www.facebook.com/premiumicaglobal
Website: www.premiumonlinehub.com

of the grounds and circumstances on which it relied to justify the use of that method.

1.5.2. Two-stage tendering

36. (1) A procurement entity shall engage in procurement by two-stage tendering

(a) where it is not feasible for the procurement entity to formulate detailed specifications for the goods or works or, in the case of services, to identify their characteristics and where it seeks tenders, proposals or offers on various means of meeting its needs in order to obtain the most satisfactory solution to its procurement needs; or where the character of the goods or works are subject to rapid technological advances;

(b) where the procurement entity seeks to enter into a contract for research, experiment, study or development, except where the contract includes the production of goods in sufficient quantities to establish their commercial viability or to recover research and development costs.

1.5.2.1. Procedures for two-stage tendering

37. (1) The provisions of Part V shall apply to two-stage tendering proceedings except to the extent that those provisions vary from this section.

(2) The invitation documents

(a) shall call upon suppliers or contractors to submit, in the first stage of two stage tendering proceedings, initial tenders which contain their proposals without a tender price;

(b) may solicit proposals that relate to technical, quality or other characteristics of the goods, works or services as well as contractual terms

TEL: +233(0)548769918 /+233 (0) 501149296
Facebook Page: www.facebook.com/premiumicaglobal
Website: www.premiumonlinehub.com

and conditions of supply and may stipulate the professional and technical competence and qualifications of the suppliers or contractors.

(3) The procurement entity may, in the first stage, engage in negotiations with any supplier or contractor whose tender has not been rejected under section 29, 32 or 62(6) with respect to any aspect of its tender.

(4) In the second stage of the two tender proceedings the procurement entity,

(a) shall invite suppliers or contractors whose tenders have not been rejected to submit final tenders with prices on a single set of specifications;

(b) may in formulating the specifications, delete or modify any aspect of the technical or quality characteristics of the goods, works or services to be procured together with any criterion originally set out in those documents, evaluate and compare tenders and ascertain the successful tender;

(c) may add new characteristics or criteria that conform with this Act;

(d) shall communicate to suppliers or contractors in the invitation to submit final tenders, any deletion, modification or addition;

(e) may permit a supplier or contractor who does not wish to submit a final tender to withdraw from the tendering proceedings without the supplier or contactor forfeiting any tender security that the supplier or contractor may have been required to provide.

(5) The final tenders shall be evaluated and compared in order to ascertain the successful tender as defined in section 59(3)(b).

TEL: +233(0)548769918 /+233 (0) 501149296
Facebook Page: www.facebook.com/premiumicaglobal
Website: www.premiumonlinehub.com

1.5.3. Restricted tendering

38. A procurement entity may for reasons of economy and efficiency and subject to the approval of the Board engage in procurement by means of restricted tendering

(a) if goods, works or services are available only from a limited number of suppliers or contractors; or

(b) if the time and cost required to examine and evaluate a large number of tenders is disproportionate to the value of the goods, works or services to be procured.

1.5.3.1. Procedure for restricted tendering

39. (1) Where a procurement entity engages in restricted tendering on the grounds referred to in section 38(a), it shall

(a) invite tenders from the suppliers and contractors who can provide the goods, works or services;

(b) select in a non-discriminatory manner, a number of suppliers or contractors to ensure effective competition.

(2) Where the procurement entity engages in restricted tendering, it shall cause a notice of the selective-tendering award to be published in the Public Procurement Bulletin.

(3) The provisions of Part V of this Act, except section 47, shall apply to selective tendering proceedings, except to the extent that those provisions are varied in this section.

1.5.4. Single-source procurement

40. (1) A procurement entity may engage in single-source procurement under section 41 with the approval of the Board,

(a) where goods, works or services are only available from a particular supplier or contractor, or if a particular supplier or contractor has

TEL: +233(0)548769918 /+233 (0) 501149296
Facebook Page: www.facebook.com/premiumicaglobal
Website: www.premiumonlinehub.com

exclusive rights in respect of the goods, works or services, and no reasonable alternative or substitute exists;

(b) where there is an urgent need for the goods, works or services and engaging in tender proceedings or any other method of procurement is impractical due to unforeseeable circumstances giving rise to the urgency which is not the result of dilatory conduct on the part of the procurement entity;

(c) where owing to a catastrophic event, there is an urgent need for the goods, works or technical services, making it impractical to use other methods of procurement because of the time involved in using those methods;

(d) where a procurement entity which has procured goods, equipment, technology or services from a supplier or contractor, determines that

(i) additional supplies need to be procured from that supplier or contractor because of standardisation;

(ii) there is a need for compatibility with existing goods, equipment, technology or services, taking into account the effectiveness of the original procurement in meeting the needs of the procurement entity;

(iii) the limited size of the proposed procurement in relation to the original procurement provides justification;

(e) where the procurement entity seeks to enter into a contract with the supplier or contractor for research, experiment, study or development, except where the contract includes the production of goods in quantities to establish commercial viability or recover research and development costs; or

(f) where the procurement entity applies this Act for procurement that concerns national security, and determines that single-source procurement is the most appropriate method of procurement.

(2) A procurement entity may engage in single-source procurement with the approval of the Board after public notice and time for comment

TEL: +233(0)548769918 /+233 (0) 501149296
Facebook Page: www.facebook.com/premiumicaglobal
Website: www.premiumonlinehub.com

where procurement from a particular supplier or contractor is necessary in order to promote a policy specified in section 59(4) (c), (d) or 69(2) (c) (i), and procurement from another supplier or contractor cannot promote that policy.

1.5.4.1. Procedure for single-source procurement

41. The procurement entity may procure the goods, works or technical services by inviting a proposal or price quotation from a single supplier or contractor under section 40.

1.5.5. Request for quotations

42. A procurement entity may engage in procurement by requesting quotations in accordance with section 43,
(a) for readily available goods or technical services that are not specially produced or provided to the particular specifications of the procurement entity; and

(b) for goods where there is an established market if the estimated value of the procurement contract is less than the amount in Schedule 3.

2. Procedure for request for quotation

43. (1) The procurement entity shall request quotations from as many suppliers or contractors as practicable, but from at least three different sources.

(2) Each supplier or contractor from whom a quotation is requested shall be informed whether any elements, apart from the charges for the goods or services themselves, such as transportation and insurance charges, customs duties and taxes, are to be included in the price.

(3) Each supplier or contractor shall only give one price quotation and shall not change its quotation;

TEL: +233(0)548769918 /+233 (0) 501149296
Facebook Page: www.facebook.com/premiumicaglobal
Website: www.premiumonlinehub.com

(4) No negotiations shall take place between the procurement entity and a supplier or contractor with respect to a quotation submitted by the supplier or contractor, prior to evaluation of bids.

3. **TENDERING PROCEDURES WITH PARTICULAR REFERENCE TO INVITATION OF TENDERS, SUBMISSION OF TENDERS AND EVALUATION AND COMPARISON OF TENDERS.**

PART V—TENDERING PROCEDURES
Sub-Part I—Invitation of Tenders and Applications to Prequalify

4. **National competitive tendering**

44. (1) In procurement proceedings in which the procurement entity decides that only domestic suppliers or contractors may submit tenders, the procurement entity shall employ national competitive tendering procedures.

(2) The procurement entity is not required to employ the procedures set out in sections 47 and 48 of this Act if the estimated contract amount is lower than the value threshold specified in Schedule 3.

(3) The procurement entity may stipulate in the tender documents that tenderers must quote only in the local currency and payments must be made wholly in the local currency.

5. **International competitive tendering**

45. (1) International competitive tendering shall be used whenever open competitive tendering is used and effective competition cannot be obtained unless foreign firms are invited to tender.

(2) Open international tendering shall be in accordance with Part IV and Part V of this Act and the following shall also apply:
(a) the invitation to tender and tender documents must be in English, subject to sections 34 and 52;

TEL: +233(0)548769918 /+233 (0) 501149296
Facebook Page: www.facebook.com/premiumicaglobal
Website: www.premiumonlinehub.com

(b) the invitation to tender shall be placed in a newspaper with adequate circulation to attract foreign competition as provided under section 47;

(c) at least six weeks shall be allowed for submission of tenders in order to allow sufficient time for the invitation to reach candidates and to enable them to prepare and submit the tenders as provided in section 53;

(d) technical specifications shall, to the extent compatible with national requirements, be based on international standards or standards widely used in international trade and in particular shall conform to the provisions of sections 33 and 50(3);

(e) tenderers are permitted to express their tenders, as well as any security documents to be presented by them, in freely convertible currency and stated in the tender documents, subject to section 50(3) and section 55(2)(c); and

(f) general and special conditions of contract as stated in the tender documents.

6. Procedures for inviting tenders or applications to prequalify

47. (1) A procurement entity shall invite tenders or, where applicable, applications to prequalify by causing an invitation to tender or an invitation to prequalify, to be published in the Procurement Bulletin.

(2) The invitation to tender or invitation to prequalify shall also be published in at least two newspapers of wide national circulation.

(3) The invitation may also be published in a newspaper of wide international circulation, in a relevant trade publication or technical or professional journal of wide international circulation.

TEL: +233(0)548769918 /+233 (0) 501149296
Facebook Page: www.facebook.com/premiumicaglobal
Website: www.premiumonlinehub.com

7. Contents of invitation to tender and invitation to prequalify

48. (1) The invitation to tender shall contain the following information:

(a) the name and address of the procurement entity;

(b) the nature, quantity and place of delivery of the goods to be supplied, the country of origin, the nature and location of the works to be effected or the nature of the technical services and the location where they are to be provided;

(c) the desired or required time for the supply of the goods or for the completion of the works, or the timetable for the provision of the services;

(d) the criteria and procedures to be used to evaluate the qualifications of suppliers or contractors, in conformity with section 23;

(e) a declaration, which may not be subsequently altered that suppliers or contractors may participate in the procurement proceedings regardless of nationality, or a declaration that participation is limited on the basis of nationality under section 25;

(f) the means of obtaining the invitation documents and the place from where they may be obtained;

(g) the price, if any, charged by the procurement entity for the invitation documents;

(h) the currency and means of payment for the invitation documents;

(i) the language in which the invitation documents are available;

(j) the place and deadline for the submission of tenders;
(k) the place, date and time for the opening of bids; and
(l) any other information considered relevant.

(2) An invitation to prequalify shall contain the information referred to in subsection (1)(a) to (e),

TEL: +233(0)548769918 /+233 (0) 501149296
Facebook Page: www.facebook.com/premiumicaglobal
Website: www.premiumonlinehub.com

(g), (h) and, if the information required under those paragraphs is already known, contain the information required under subsection (1) (j), as well as the following information

(a) the means to obtain the pre-qualification documents and the place from where they can be obtained;

(b) the price charged by the procurement entity for the pre-qualification documents;

(c) the currency and terms of payment for the pre-qualification documents;

(d) the language in which the pre-qualification documents are available;

(e) the place and deadline for the submission of applications to prequalify and the time allowed for the preparation of pre-qualification applications shall not be less than four weeks.

8. Provision of tender documents

49. (1) The procurement entity shall provide the tender documents to suppliers or contractors in accordance with the procedures and requirements specified in the invitation to tender.

(2) If pre-qualification proceedings have taken place, the procurement entity shall provide a set of tender documents to each supplier or contractor that has been prequalified and that pays the price charged for those documents.

(3) The price that the procurement entity may charge for the tender documents shall reflect the cost of printing them and providing them to suppliers or contractors.

TEL: +233(0)548769918 /+233 (0) 501149296
Facebook Page: www.facebook.com/premiumicaglobal
Website: www.premiumonlinehub.com

9. Contents of tender documents and use of standard tender documents

50. (1) Procurement entities shall use the appropriate standard tender documents stipulated in Schedule 4 with such minimum changes acceptable to the Board.

(2) Changes shall be introduced only through tender or contract data sheets, or through special conditions of contract and not by introducing changes in the standard tender documents.

(3) The invitation documents shall include,
(a) instructions for preparing tenders;
(b) the criteria and procedures, in conformity with the provisions of section 22, for the evaluation of the qualifications of suppliers or contractors;
(c) the requirements on additional documentary evidence or other information that is to be submitted by suppliers or contractors to demonstrate their qualifications;

(d) the nature and required technical and quality characteristics, in relation to the goods, works or technical services to be procured under section 33 including, but not limited to,

(i) technical specifications, plans, drawings and designs,
(ii) the quantity of the goods;
(iii) any incidental services to be performed;
(iv) the location where the works is to be effected or the services are to be provided; and
(v) the desired or required time, if any when the goods are to be delivered, the construction is to be effected or the services are to be provided;
(e) the criteria to be used by the procurement entity to determine the successful tender, including any margin of preference and any criteria other than price to be used under section 59(4)(b)(c) or (d) and the factors apart from price to be used to determine the lowest evaluated bid, shall, to the extent practicable, be expressed in monetary terms, or given a relative weight in the evaluation provisions in the tender documents;

TEL: +233(0)548769918 /+233 (0) 501149296
Facebook Page: www.facebook.com/premiumicaglobal
Website: www.premiumonlinehub.com

(f) the terms and conditions of the procurement contract and the contract form to be signed by the parties;

(g) a statement that the characteristics of the goods, works or services, contractual terms and conditions or other requirements set out in the invitation documents are permitted, and a description of the manner in which alternative tenders are to be evaluated and compared;

(h) a description of the portion or portions for which tenders may be submitted where suppliers or contractors are permitted to submit tenders for only a portion of the goods, works or services to be procured;

(i) the manner in which the tender price is to be formulated and expressed, including a statement whether the price covers elements apart from the goods, works or services, such as applicable transportation and insurance charges, customs duties and taxes;

(j) the currency or currencies in which the tender price is to be formulated and expressed;

(k) the language in conformity with section 52, in which tenders are to be prepared;

(l) any requirements of

(i) the procurement entity connected with the issue, nature, form, amount and other principal terms and conditions of tender security to be provided by suppliers or contractors submitting tenders; and

(ii) security for the performance of the procurement contract to be provided by a supplier or contractor that enters into the procurement contract, including securities such as labour and materials bonds;

(m) a statement that a supplier or contractor can modify or withdraw its tender prior to the deadline for the submission of tenders without forfeiting its tender security;

(n) the manner, place and deadline for the submission of tenders;

(o) the means by which suppliers or contractors may seek clarification of the invitation documents and a statement whether the procurement entity intends to convene a meeting of suppliers or contractors;

(p) the period of time during which tenders will be in effect;

(q) the place, date and time for the opening of tenders;

(r) the procedures to be followed for opening and examining tenders;

(s) the currency that will be used to evaluate and compare tenders under section 58 and either the exchange rate that will be used for the conversion of tenders into that currency or a statement that the rate

TEL: +233(0)548769918 /+233 (0) 501149296
Facebook Page: www.facebook.com/premiumicaglobal
Website: www.premiumonlinehub.com

published by a specified financial institution prevailing on a specified date will be used;

(t) references to this Act, the procurement regulations and other Acts and regulations relevant to the procurement proceedings, but the omission of the reference shall not constitute grounds for review under Part VII or give rise to liability on the part of the procurement entity;

(u) the name, functional title and address of one or more officers or employees of the procurement entity who are authorised to communicate directly with and to receive communications directly from a supplier or contractor in connection with the procurement proceedings, without the intervention of an intermediary;

(v) any commitments to be made by the supplier or contractor outside the procurement contract, such as commitments relating to countertrade or to the transfer of technology;

(w) a statement of the right to seek review of an unlawful act or decision of, or procedure followed by the procurement entity in relation to the procurement proceedings;

(x) if the procurement entity reserves the right to reject tenders, a statement to that effect;

(y) any formalities that will be required once a tender has been accepted, for a procurement contract to enter into force, including, where applicable, the execution of a written procurement contract and approval by the
Government and the estimated period of time following the despatch of the notice of acceptance that will be required to obtain the approval; and

(z) any other requirements established by the procurement entity under this Act and Regulations relating to the preparation and submission of tenders and to other aspects of the procurement proceedings.

TEL: +233(0)548769918 /+233 (0) 501149296
Facebook Page: www.facebook.com/premiumicaglobal
Website: www.premiumonlinehub.com

10. Clarifications and modifications of tender documents

51. (1) A supplier or contractor may request promptly clarification of the tender documents from the procurement entity.

(2) The procurement entity shall respond to a request by a supplier or contractor within a reasonable time before the deadline for the submission of tenders to enable the supplier or contractor make a timely submission of its tender and shall without disclosing the source of the request communicate the clarification to the suppliers or contractors provided with the invitation documents.

(3) The procurement entity may modify the invitation documents by issuing an addendum (textual matter added onto a publication or document; usually at the end) prior to the deadline for submission of tenders.

(4) The addendum shall be communicated promptly to the suppliers or contractors provided with the invitation documents by the procurement entity and shall be binding on those suppliers or contractors.

(5) The procurement entity may convene a meeting of suppliers and contractors to clarify and modify tender documents and shall prepare minutes of any previous meeting concerned with clarification of the invitation documents without identifying the sources of the requests.
(6) The minutes shall be given promptly to the suppliers and contractors provided with the invitation documents by the procurement entity to enable them take the minutes into account in the preparation of their tenders.

11. Submission of tenders

53. (1) The procurement entity shall,
(a) fix the place for, and a specific date and time as the deadline for the submission of tenders; and
(b) allow tenderers at least six weeks to prepare their tenders for international competitive tendering.

TEL: +233(0)548769918 /+233 (0) 501149296
Facebook Page: www.facebook.com/premiumicaglobal
Website: www.premiumonlinehub.com

(2) The time for preparation of tenders under national competitive tendering procedures shall not exceed four weeks.

(3) If a procurement entity issues clarification or modification documents or if a meeting of tenderers is held, the procurement entity shall prior to the expiry of the deadline for the submission of tenders extend the deadline to give the suppliers and contractors reasonable time to take the clarification or modification, or the minutes of the meeting into account in their tenders.

(4) The procurement entity may, prior to the expiry of deadline for the submission of tenders, extend the deadline.

(5) The procurement entity shall, at least ten days before the expiry of the deadline, give notice of an extension of the deadline by fax, e-mail or any other expedited written means of communication to each supplier or contractor to whom the procurement entity provided the tender documents or to any new prospective tenderers.

(6) A tender shall be in writing, signed and be submitted in a sealed envelope.

(7) A tender may alternatively be submitted in any other form specified in the tender documents that provides a record of the contents of the tender and a similar degree of authenticity, security and confidentiality.

(8) The procurement entity shall provide the tenderer with a receipt showing the date and time when it's tender was received.

(9) A tender received by the procurement entity after the deadline for the submission of tenders shall not be opened and shall be returned to the supplier or contractor which submitted it.

TEL: +233(0)548769918 /+233 (0) 501149296
Facebook Page: www.facebook.com/premiumicaglobal
Website: www.premiumonlinehub.com

12. Examination of tenders

57. (1) The procurement entity may ask a supplier or a contractor for clarification of its tender in order to assist in the examination, evaluation and comparison of tenders.

(2) No change in a matter of substance in the tender, including changes in price and changes aimed at making an unresponsive tender responsive, shall be sought, offered or permitted.

(3) Notwithstanding subsection (2), the procurement entity shall correct purely arithmetical errors that are discovered during the examination of tenders.

(4) The procurement entity shall give prompt notice of the correction to the supplier or contractor that submitted the tender.

13. Evaluation of tenders

59. (1) The procurement entity shall evaluate and compare the tenders that have been accepted in order to ascertain the successful tender in accordance with the procedures and criteria set out in the invitation documents.

(2) No criterion shall be used that has not been set out in the invitation documents.

(3) The successful tender shall be:
(a) the tender with the lowest evaluated tender price; and
(b) the lowest evaluated tender ascertained on the basis of criteria specified in the invitation documents which shall be

(i) objective and quantifiable; and
(ii) given relative weight in the evaluation procedure or expressed in monetary terms where practicable if the procurement entity has so stipulated in the invitation documents.

(4) To determine the lowest evaluated tender, the procurement entity shall consider

TEL: +233(0)548769918 /+233 (0) 501149296
Facebook Page: www.facebook.com/premiumicaglobal
Website: www.premiumonlinehub.com

(a) the tender price, subject to any margin of preference applied under section
60(2) ;

(b) the cost of operating, maintaining and repairing the goods or works, the time for delivery of the goods, completion of works or provisions of the services, the functional characteristics of the goods or works, the terms of payment and of guarantees in respect of the goods, works or services;

(c) the effect the acceptance of the tender will have on

(i) the balance of payments position and foreign exchange reserves of the country;
(ii) the countertrade arrangements offered by suppliers or contractors;
(iii) the extent of local content, including manufacturer, labour and materials, in goods, works or services being offered by suppliers or contractors;
(iv) the economic-development potential offered by tenders, including domestic investment or other business activity;
(v) the encouragement of employment, the reservation of certain production for domestic suppliers;
(vi) the transfer of technology;
(vii) the development of managerial, scientific and operational skills; and
(d) national security considerations.

14. Acceptance of tender and entry into force of procurement contract

65. (1) A tender that has been ascertained to be the successful tender in accordance with this Act shall be accepted and notice of acceptance of the tender shall be given within 30 days of the acceptance of the tender to the supplier or contractor submitting the tender.

(2) Where the tender documents require the supplier or contractor whose tender has been accepted to sign a written procurement contract conforming to the tender, the procurement entity and the supplier or contractor shall sign the procurement contract within 30 days after the

TEL: +233(0)548769918 /+233 (0) 501149296
Facebook Page: www.facebook.com/premiumicaglobal
Website: www.premiumonlinehub.com

notice referred to in subsection (1) is despatched to the supplier or contractor.

(3) Where a written procurement contract is required to be signed, the contract shall enter into force on the commencement date indicated on the contract.

(4) Between the time when the notice is despatched to the supplier or contractor and the entry into force of the procurement contract, neither the procurement entity nor the supplier or contractor shall take any action that interferes with the entry into force of the procurement contract or with its performance.

(5) Except as provided in subsection (2), a procurement contract in accordance with the terms and conditions of the accepted tender enters into force when the notice is despatched to the supplier or contractor that submitted the tender, if it is despatched while the tender is in force.

(6) The notice is despatched when it is properly addressed or otherwise directed and transmitted to the supplier or contractor or conveyed to an appropriate authority for transmission to the supplier or contractor in a manner authorised in section 26.

(7) If the supplier or contractor whose tender has been accepted fails to sign a written procurement contract within 30 working days of receipt of the notice of acceptance or fails to provide the required security for the performance of the contract, the procurement entity shall select a successful tender in accordance with section 59(3) from among the remaining tenders that are in force, subject to the right of the procurement entity to reject the remaining tenders.

(8) The notice provided for in subsection (1) shall be given to the supplier or contractor that submitted the successful tender.

(9) A procurement entity shall give notice of the procurement contract in writing to unsuccessful suppliers and contractors and the notice shall
(a) specify the name and address of the successful supplier or contractor who has entered into the contract and the contract price;

TEL: +233(0)548769918 /+233 (0) 501149296
Facebook Page: www.facebook.com/premiumicaglobal
Website: www.premiumonlinehub.com

(b) be given after the commencement of the procurement contract and may include the provision by the supplier or contractor of security for the performance of the contract;

(c) for contracts above the threshold in Schedule 3, be published in the Procurement Bulletin which shall disclose the names of firms or individuals awarded contracts, the start and completion dates, as well as the value of the contracts.

15. METHODS AND PROCEDURES FOR ENGAGING THE SERVICES OF CONSULTANTS.

PART VI—METHODS AND PROCEDURES TO PROCURE CONSULTANTS

16. Notice of invitation of expressions of interest and preparation of shortlists

66. (1) A procurement entity shall invite consulting services by causing a notice seeking expression of interest in submitting a proposal to be published in the Public
Procurement Bulletin for consultancy contracts above the threshold in Schedule 3.

(2) The notice shall,

(a) contain the name and address of the procurement entity and a brief description of the services to be procured; and

(b) be published in English and in a newspaper of wide circulation or in a relevant trade or professional publication of wide circulation except where participation is limited solely to national consultants under section 44 (1) or where the procurement entity decides that only national consultants may submit proposals.

(3) Where direct invitation is necessary for economic and efficiency reasons, the procurement entity with the approval of the Board may apply the provisions of subsection (1) and (2) where

(a) the services to be procured are available only from a limited number of consultants, if it invites expressions of interest from all these consultants;

(b) the time and cost required to examine and evaluate a large number of expressions of interest would be disproportionate to the value of the

TEL: +233(0)548769918 /+233 (0) 501149296
Facebook Page: www.facebook.com/premiumicaglobal
Website: www.premiumonlinehub.com

services to be performed, if it invites proposals from enough consultants to ensure effective competition; or

(c) direct invitation is the only means to ensure confidentiality or is required in the national interest, if it invites enough proposals from consultants for effective competition.

17. Content of requests for proposals for consultancy services

68. (1) The procurement entity shall use the standard invitation for proposals stipulated in Schedule 4 and any requirements for a specific assignment shall be introduced through information to consultants, data sheets or contract data sheets and not by introducing changes in the standard tender documents.

(2) The invitation for proposals shall include
(a) the name and address of the procurement entity;
(b) the language or languages in which proposals are to be prepared;
(c) the manner, place and deadline for the submission of proposals;
(d) a statement to the effect that the procurement entity reserves the right to reject proposals;
(e) the criteria and procedures related to the evaluation of the qualifications of the consultants and those related to additional qualifications under section
24(5);
(f) the requirements on documentary evidence or other information that shall be submitted by suppliers or contractors to demonstrate their qualifications;
(g) the nature and required characteristics of the services to be procured including the location where the services are to be provided and the time when the services are to be provided;
(h) whether the procurement entity is seeking proposals on various possible ways of meeting its needs;
(i) the currency in which the proposal price is to be expressed;
(j) the manner in which the proposal price is to be expressed, including a statement on whether the price covers elements apart from the cost of services, such as reimbursement for transportation, lodging, insurance, use of equipment, duties or taxes;

TEL: +233(0)548769918 /+233 (0) 501149296
Facebook Page: www.facebook.com/premiumicaglobal
Website: www.premiumonlinehub.com

(k) the procedure selected under section 71(1) to ascertain the successful proposal;

(l) the criteria to be used to determine the successful proposal, including any margin of preference to be used under section 57 and the relative weight of the criteria;

(m) the currency that will be used to evaluate and compare proposals and either the exchange rate that will be used for the conversion of proposal prices into that currency or a statement that the rate published by a specified financial institution prevailing on a specified date will be used;

(n) a statement on alternatives to the characteristics of the consultancy services, contractual terms and conditions or other requirements set out in the invitation for proposals if permitted and a description of the manner in which the alternative proposals are to be evaluated and compared;

(o) the name, functional title and address of one or more officers or employees of the procurement entity who are authorised to communicate directly with and to receive communications directly from consultants in connection with the procurement proceedings, without the intervention of an intermediary;

(p) the means by which consultants may seek clarification on the invitation for proposals and a statement whether the procurement entity intends to convene a meeting of consultants; and

(q) the terms and conditions of the consultancy contract as known to the procurement entity and the contract form to be signed by the parties.

18. Criteria for the evaluation of proposals

69. (1) The procurement entity shall establish criteria to evaluate the proposals and determine the relative weight to be accorded to each criterion and the manner in which they are to be applied in the evaluation of proposals.

(2) The consultants shall be notified of the criteria in the invitation for proposals and the criteria may deal with the following:

(a) the qualifications, experience, reputation, reliability and professional and managerial competence of the consultant and the personnel to be involved in providing the services;

TEL: +233(0)548769918 /+233 (0) 501149296
Facebook Page: www.facebook.com/premiumicaglobal
Website: www.premiumonlinehub.com

(b) the effectiveness of the proposals submitted by the consultants in meeting the needs of the procurement entity as specified in section 68(2)(g);

(c) the proposal price, including any ancillary or related costs; and

(i) the effect that the acceptance of a proposal will have on the balance of payments position and foreign exchange reserves of the country;

(ii) the extent of participation by nationals;

(iii) the economic development potential offered by the proposal, including domestic investment or other business activity;

(iv) the encouragement of employment;

(v) the transfer of technology;

(vi) the development of managerial, scientific and operational skills;

(vii) the counter-trade arrangements offered by consultants; and

(d) national security considerations.

(3) A procurement entity may grant additional points for participation by nationals who are key staff in foreign and national firms, and these points shall be calculated in accordance with the procurement regulations and reflected in the record of the procurement proceedings subject to approval by the Board.

19. Clarification and modification of invitation for proposals

70. (1) A consultant may request clarification of the invitation for proposals from the procurement entity and where such a request is made the procurement entity shall

(a) respond to the request within 7 working days of the request being made if the request is received by the procurement entity within 14 working days prior to the deadline for the submission of proposals; and

(b) where the request is made later than 14 days prior to the deadline for the submission of proposals, respond promptly and early enough to enable the consultant make a timely submission of its proposal and shall, without identifying the source of the invitation, communicate the clarification to the other consultants to whom the procurement entity has provided the invitation for proposals.

TEL: +233(0)548769918 /+233 (0) 501149296
Facebook Page: www.facebook.com/premiumicaglobal
Website: www.premiumonlinehub.com

(2) A procurement entity may, whether on its initiative or as a result of a request for clarification by a consultant, modify the request for proposals by issuing an addendum at any time prior to the deadline for the submission of proposals.

(3) The addendum shall be communicated promptly before the deadline for the submission of proposals to the short-listed consultants to whom the procurement entity has provided the request for proposals and shall be binding on those consultants.

(4) If the procurement entity convenes a meeting of consultants, it shall prepare minutes of the meeting containing the requests submitted at the meeting for clarification of the request for proposal and its responses to those requests, without identifying the sources of the requests.

(5) The minutes shall be provided promptly before the deadline for the submission of proposals to the consultants participating in the selection proceedings to enable them take the minutes into account in preparing their proposals.

20. Choice of selection procedure

71. (1) The procurement entity shall use the selection procedure provided for in section 75(6)(a), 75(6)(b) or 76 that has been notified to consultants in the invitation for proposals.

(2) The procurement entity shall include in the record required under section 28, a statement of the grounds and circumstances on which it relied to justify the use of a selection procedure under subsection (1).

(3) This Part does not prevent a procurement entity from resorting to an impartial panel of external experts in the selection procedure.

TEL: +233(0)548769918 /+233 (0) 501149296
Facebook Page: www.facebook.com/premiumicaglobal
Website: www.premiumonlinehub.com

21. Evaluation of proposals

74. (1) The evaluation of the proposals shall be carried out in two stages: first the quality, and then the cost.
(2) Evaluators of technical proposals should not have access to the financial proposals until the technical evaluation, including any Tender Board Reviews is concluded.
(3) The evaluation shall be carried out in conformity with the provisions in the invitation for proposals.

22. Selection procedure where price is a factor

75. (1) Where the procurement entity uses the procedure in this section, it shall establish a threshold on the quality and technical aspects of the proposals in accordance with the criteria established under section 69 apart from those set out in the request for proposals and shall rate each proposal in accordance with that criteria and the relative weight and manner of application of those criteria set out in the invitation for proposals.

(2) The procurement entity shall notify the consultants whose proposals did not meet the minimum qualifying mark or were non responsive to the invitation for proposals and terms of reference after the evaluation of quality is completed within a period of 14 days after the decision has been taken by the procurement entity.

(3) The name of the consultant, the quality scores and the proposed prices shall be read aloud and recorded when the financial proposals are opened.

(4) The procurement entity shall prepare the minutes of public opening of financial proposals which shall be part of the evaluation report and shall retain this record.

(5) The procurement entity shall compare the prices of the proposals that have attained a rating at or above the threshold.

(6) The successful proposals shall be

TEL: +233(0)548769918 /+233 (0) 501149296
Facebook Page: www.facebook.com/premiumicaglobal
Website: www.premiumonlinehub.com

(a) the proposals with the best combined evaluation in terms of the criteria established under section 69 apart from price in the case of quality and cost - based selection;
(b) the proposals with the lowest price in the case of least-cost selection; or
(c) the consultants that submitted the highest ranked technical proposals within the budget;

(7) The consultants with the winning proposals shall be invited for negotiations, which shall focus mainly on the technical proposals.
(8) Proposed unit rates for staff-months and reimbursable shall not be negotiated unless there are exceptional reasons.

23. Selection procedure where price is not a factor

76. (1) Where the procurement entity uses the quality-based selection, selection based on consultant's qualifications or single-source selection, it shall engage in negotiations with consultants in accordance with this section.

(2) The procurement entity shall

(a) establish a threshold in accordance with section 75(1);
(b) invite for negotiations on the price of its proposal, the consultant that has attained the best rating in accordance with section 75(1);
(c) inform the consultants that attained ratings above the threshold that they may be considered for negotiation if the negotiations with the consultant with the best rating do not result in a procurement contract; and
(d) inform the consultant with the best rating, that it is terminating the negotiations if it becomes apparent to the procurement entity that the negotiations with that consultant invited under subsection (2)(b), will not result in a procurement contract.

(3) The procurement entity shall, if negotiations with the consultant with the best rating fails, invite the consultant that obtained the second best rating, and if the negotiations with that consultant do not result in a procurement contract, the procurement entity shall invite the other

TEL: +233(0)548769918 /+233 (0) 501149296
Facebook Page: www.facebook.com/premiumicaglobal
Website: www.premiumonlinehub.com

consultants for negotiations on the basis of their rating until it arrives at a contract or rejects the remaining proposals.

24. REVIEW PROCEDURES UNDER THE PUBLIC PROCUREMENT ACT.

PART VII—REVIEW

25. Right to review

78. (1) Any supplier, contractor or consultant that claims to have suffered, or that may suffer loss or injury due to a breach of a duty imposed on the procurement entity by this
Act, may seek review in accordance with this Part.

(2) Notwithstanding subsection (1), the following shall not be subject to the review
(a) the selection of a method of procurement under sections 35 to 43;
(b) the choice of a selection procedure under section 75(6) (a), 75(6) (b) or section 76;
(c) the limitation of procurement proceedings in accordance with section 44; and
(d) a decision by the procurement entity under section 29 to reject tenders, proposals, offers or quotation.

26. Review by procurement entity

79. (1) A complaint shall, in the first instance, be submitted in writing to the head of the procurement entity if the procurement contract has not already entered into force.

(2) The head of the procurement entity shall not entertain a complaint unless it was submitted within twenty days after the supplier, contractor or consultant submitting it became aware of the circumstances giving rise to the complaint or when that supplier, contractor, or consultant should have become aware of those circumstances, whichever is earlier.

(3) The head of the procurement entity may entertain a complaint or continue to entertain a complaint after the procurement contract has entered into force notwithstanding subsection (1).

TEL: +233(0)548769918 /+233 (0) 501149296
Facebook Page: www.facebook.com/premiumicaglobal
Website: www.premiumonlinehub.com

(4) A procurement entity shall attempt to resolve a complaint by mutual agreement of the supplier or contractor and the procurement entity.

(5) The head of the procurement entity shall, within twenty-one days after the submission of the complaint, issue a written decision.

(6) The decision shall
(a) state the reasons for the decision; and
(b) if the complaint is upheld in whole or in part, indicate the corrective measures that are to be taken.

(7) If the head of the procurement entity does not issue a decision by the time specified in subsection

(5), the supplier, contractor, or consultant, submitting the complaint is entitled to institute proceedings for administrative review under section 80.

(8) After the institution of the proceedings, the competence of the head of the procuring entity to entertain the complaint ceases.

27. Administrative review

80. (1) A supplier, contractor or consultant entitled to seek review may submit a complaint to the Board,
(a) within twenty-one days after

(i) the supplier, contractor or consultant became aware of the circumstances giving rise to the complaint; or

(ii) the time when the supplier, contractor or consultant ought to have become aware of those circumstances, if the complaint cannot be submitted under section 79 because of the entry into force of the procurement contract;

(b) if the head of the procurement entity does not entertain the complaint because the procurement contract has entered into force, and the

TEL: +233(0)548769918 /+233 (0) 501149296
Facebook Page: www.facebook.com/premiumicaglobal
Website: www.premiumonlinehub.com

complaint is submitted within twenty-one days after the issuance of the decision not to entertain the complaint;

(c) under section 79(7) if the complaint is submitted within twenty-one days after the expiry of the period referred to in section 79(5); or

(d) if the supplier, contractor, or consultant claims to be adversely affected by a decision of the head of the procurement entity under section 79, and the complaint is submitted within twenty days after the issue of the decision.

(2) Upon receipt of a complaint, the Board shall give notice of the complaint promptly to the procurement entity.

(3) The Board may,
(a) declare the legal rules or principles that govern the subject-matter of the complaint;
(b) order that the provisions of this Act be complied with;
(c) require the procurement entity that has acted or proceeded in an illegal manner, or that has reached an illegal decision, to act or to proceed in a legal manner or to reach a legal decision;
(d) annul in whole or in part an illegal act or decision of the procurement entity, other than any act or decision bringing the procurement contract into force;
(e) revise an illegal decision by the procurement entity or substitute its own decision for the decision, other than any decision bringing the procurement contract into force;
(f) require the payment of compensation for reasonable costs incurred by the supplier or contractor who submitted the complaint, in connection with the procurement proceedings as a result of an illegal decision of, or procedure followed by the procurement entity;
(g) order that the procurement proceedings be terminated;
(h) dismiss the complaint and require the payment of compensation for reasonable costs incurred by the Procurement Entity or the Board.

(4) The Board shall, within twenty-one days of starting a review, issue a written decision concerning the complaint, stating the reasons for the decision.

TEL: +233(0)548769918 /+233 (0) 501149296
Facebook Page: www.facebook.com/premiumicaglobal
Website: www.premiumonlinehub.com

(5) Correspondence pertaining to any complaint shall be copied to the Board.

28. Certain rules applicable to review proceedings

81. (1) The head of the procurement entity or the Board shall notify the suppliers, contractors, or consultants participating in procurement proceedings about the submission of a complaint and of its substance within 14 working days after the submission of the complaint for review.

(2) A supplier or contractor or any government authority whose interests are or could be affected by the review proceedings is entitled to participate in the review proceedings.

(3) A supplier, contractor, or consultant who fails to participate in the review proceedings is barred from subsequently making the same type of claim.

(4) A copy of the decision of the head of the procurement entity or of the Board shall be furnished within five days after the issue of the decision to the supplier, contractor, or consultant submitting the complaint to the procurement entity and to any other supplier, contractor or government authority that has participated in the review proceedings.

(5) After the decision has been taken, the complaint and the decision shall be promptly made available for inspection by the general public, but no information shall be disclosed if its disclosure would be contrary to law, would impede law enforcement, would not be in the public interest, would prejudice legitimate commercial interests of the parties or would inhibit fair competition.

TEL: +233(0)548769918 /+233 (0) 501149296
Facebook Page: www.facebook.com/premiumicaglobal
Website: www.premiumonlinehub.com

29. Suspension of procurement proceedings

82. (1) Where review proceedings are initiated, the procurement proceedings may be suspended for 7 days if the complaint
(a) is not frivolous;
(b) contains a declaration which demonstrates that the supplier, contractor or consultant will suffer irreparable damage if the suspension is not granted; and
(d) is likely to succeed and the grant of the suspension will not cause disproportionate harm to the procurement entity or to other suppliers, contractors, or consultants.

(2) When the procurement contract enters into force, upon the submission of a complaint under section 79, performance of the procurement contract shall be suspended for seven days, if the complaint meets the requirements set out in subsection (1).

(3) The head of the procurement entity and the Board under subsection (2) may extend the suspension in order to preserve the rights of the supplier, contractor, or consultant who is a party to the review pending the disposition of the review proceedings, but the total period of suspension shall not exceed thirty days.

(4) The suspension provided for by this section shall not apply if the procurement entity certifies that urgent public interest considerations requires the procurement to proceed.
(5) The certification shall state the grounds for the finding that urgent considerations exist and shall be made a part of the record of the procurement proceedings, and it is conclusive with respect to administrative review.

(6) Any decision by the procurement entity under this section and the grounds and circumstances shall be made part of the record of the procurement proceedings.

30. PROCEDURE FOR DISPOSAL OF STORES, PLANT AND EQUIPMENT.

PART VIII—DISPOSAL OF STORES, PLANT AND EQUIPMENT

31. Authority to dispose

83. (1) The head of a procurement entity shall convene a Board of Survey comprising representatives of departments with unserviceable, obsolete or surplus stores, plant and equipment which shall report on the items and subject to a technical report on them, recommend the best method of disposal after the officer in charge has completed a Board of Survey form.

(2) The Board of Survey's recommendations shall be approved by the head of the procurement entity and the items shall be disposed of as approved.

(3) Where items become unserviceable for reasons other than fair wear and tear, such as through accident or expiry, a set procedure established by the Board for handling losses shall be followed before the items are boarded and disposed of.

32. Disposal procedures

84. Disposal of obsolete and surplus items shall be by
(a) transfer to government departments or other public entities, with or without financial adjustment;
(b) sale by public tender to the highest tenderer, subject to reserve price;
(c) sale by public auction, subject to a reserve price; or
(d) destruction, dumping, or burying as appropriate.

33. Procedure for procurement at the District Assembly level

1. Storekeeper, State Officer or Heads of Spending Units raises requisitions by completing the Activity & Expenditure Initiation forms. Heads of MDAs or Directors Finance & Administration approves the requests.

TEL: +233(0)548769918 /+233 (0) 501149296
Facebook Page: www.facebook.com/premiumicaglobal
Website: www.premiumonlinehub.com

2. Procurement Officer makes request for quotations by inviting bids or collecting Pro- forma Invoice from potential suppliers (at least 3). The relevant current procurement procedures must be used.

3. The Tender Committee reviews the bids and selects a supplier.

4. The Procurement Officer prepares the Purchase Order (PO) and forwards it to the Accountant who ensures that the transaction has been properly charged to the appropriate expenditure account.

5. The Accountant then authorises the purchase and the Head of MDA (Director Finance & Administration, Director General, Chief Director, Deputy Minister or Minister approves the PO. This process commits the transaction against the Budget Allocation (Warrant) of the MDA.

6. For the MDAs on the manual system, the signed PO should be submitted to the Servicing Treasury for final commitment before it is issued to the suppliers.

7. Goods are delivered to the Storekeepers and inspected by a team including the Internal Auditor. The Store Receipt Advice are then prepared and signed.

i. **Allocated Stores**: are those costs that are allocated to and remain a charge to the sub-head of expenditure for which funds are provided in the estimates. They may be either purchased directly or obtained from the unallocated stores stock.

ii. **Unallocated Stores** are those items purchased for general stock rather than for a particular work or service for which the final vote of charge cannot be stated at the time of purchase.

iii. **Expandable Stores**: are items purchased for use to replace existing ones been used currently when they are worn out. E.g. Shovels, pick-axes, brushes, brooms

TEL: +233(0)548769918 /+233 (0) 501149296
Facebook Page: www.facebook.com/premiumicaglobal
Website: www.premiumonlinehub.com

iv.   **Consumable Stores:** are items purchased for daily use by the government organization. E.g. stationery, soap, tyres, fuel spare parts,

v.   **Un-expandable Stores:** are stocks purchased for use over a long period of time and it is of capital nature. E.g. plant & machinery, motor vehicles

34. WEAKNESSES OF THE PUBLIC PROCUREMENT IN GHANA

The procurement Act of Ghana, Act 663 (2003), was enacted and promulgated by parliament of the republic of Ghana to, among other things; **bring sanity and conformity to public procurement by instituting bodies and principles that harmonizes the public procurement process and activities.**

Even though the Act is good, it has some disadvantages which may include the following:
1. Lack of Clear Procedure for Emergency Procurement
2. Slow Pace in Regularizing the Draft Regulations
3. Lack of Qualified Procurement Personnel
4. High Cost of Advertisement

TEL: +233(0)548769918 /+233 (0) 501149296
Facebook Page: www.facebook.com/premiumicaglobal
Website: www.premiumonlinehub.com

SUMMARY - PUBLIC PROCUREMENT

Public Procurement refers to the process through which goods, services and works are financed either wholly or in part by public institutions (MDAs/MMDAs) for public purposes.

Public Procurement is governed by an Act of Parliament called the Public Procurement Act, 2003 and led by a Board with a Chief Executive Officer and a Minister of Procurement.

➢ ***Scope of Application of the Act***

- *The Act applies to the procurement of goods, works and services financed in whole or in part from public funds except where the Minister decides that it is in the National interest to use a different procedure.*

- *It applies to:*
  - *Central management agencies*
  - *Ministries, Departments and Agencies (MDAs)*
  - *Subvented agencies; these are organizations funded by government to undertake projects.*
  - *Government institutions*
  - *Public Universities, public schools, colleges and hospitals*
  - *Bank of Ghana*
  - *Among others.*

TEL: +233(0)548769918 /+233 (0) 501149296
Facebook Page: www.facebook.com/premiumicaglobal
Website: www.premiumonlinehub.com

➢ **Structure of the Public Procurement**

The structure of the Public Procurement in Ghana is as follows:

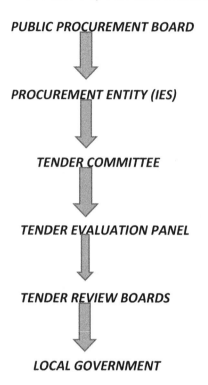

PUBLIC PROCUREMENT BOARD

PROCUREMENT ENTITY (IES)

TENDER COMMITTEE

TENDER EVALUATION PANEL

TENDER REVIEW BOARDS

LOCAL GOVERNMENT

a. **Functions of the Public Procurement Authority**

The Public Procurement Authority (Board) oversees the entire Public Procurement in Ghana. Below are some of the functions of the Board:

- *Make proposal for the formulation of policies on procurement*
- *Monitor and supervise public procurement in the country*
- *Development of Public Procurement documents (rules, directives, instructions, other regulations)*
- *Preparation and presentation to annual report on procurement*
- *Government advisor on public procurement issues*
- *Maintenance of public procurement entities.*

TEL: +233(0)548769918 /+233 (0) 501149296
Facebook Page: www.facebook.com/premiumicaglobal
Website: www.premiumonlinehub.com

What the Public Procurement Authority does not do:

- *Procure for or on behalf of any Government Entity*
- *Award any contract for or on behalf of any Government Entity*
- *Invite tenders for or on behalf of any Government Entity*

Expenses of the Board; *Parliament through appropriation grants the Board with such money as it may require.*

Accounts and Audit; *The Board shall keep records and prepare annual accounts as prescribed by the Controller and Accountant General and approved by the Auditor General.*

    b. **Procurement Entity:**

A Procurement entity is responsible for procurement of goods, services and works.

The Minister may in consultation with the Board by notice in the Gazette declare any entity or individual to be a procurement entity and shall carry out its duties as laid down in this Act or by the Board.

    c. **Tender Committee:**

Each Procurement Entity shall have a Tender Committee that will be responsible for:

- *Ensuring that each stage of the Procurement activities in this Act and recommended by the Board.*
- *Ensuring that the Procurement Entities exercise sound judgment in making procurement decisions*
- *Referring to appropriate Tender Review Board for approval beyond its authority.*

TEL: +233(0)548769918 /+233 (0) 501149296
Facebook Page: www.facebook.com/premiumicaglobal
Website: www.premiumonlinehub.com

d. **Tender Evaluation Panel**

- *This Panel has the expertise to evaluate tenders and assess the Tender Committee in its work.*
- *They shall evaluate each tender according to the pre-determined and publish evaluation criteria.*

e. **Tender Review Boards (TRB)**

At each level of the Procurement process, the TPB is established;

- *Central TRB*
- *Ministerial TRB*
- *Regional TRB*
- *District TRB*

NOTE: *The Public Procurement (Amendment) Act 2016 (Act 914) has brought dissolution of District and Ministerial for TRB.*

Functions

- *Approval of the Procurement process by the Procurement Entity*
- *Furnish the Procurement Board with annual report*
- *Participate in Public Procurement forums*
- *Review the decisions of heads of entities in respect of a complaints.*

➢ **Procurement Plan**

A Procurement Entity prepares a Procurement Plan and submits its approved programmes and plan for approval by the Tender Committee and shall indicate:

- Contract packages
- Estimated cost for each contract packages
- The procurement methods
- Processing steps and time
- Among others

TEL: +233(0)548769918 /+233 (0) 501149296
Facebook Page: www.facebook.com/premiumicaglobal
Website: www.premiumonlinehub.com

➤ **Qualification of Tenderers**

A tenderer in Public Procurement shall

a. Possess the necessary
   - Professional and technical qualifications and competences
   - Financial resources
   - Equipment and other physical facilities
b. Have the legal capacity to enter the contract
c. Be solvent; not bankrupt
d. Pay taxes
e. Directors of the tenders are qualified and not declared bankrupt or illegal behavior
f. Pay Social Security Fund and pay all compensation for pollution if any.

➤ **Pre – qualification Procurement**

A Procurement Entity may engage in pre- qualification proceeding to identify tenderer who are qualified prior to the submission of tenders.

➤ **Rejection of tenders, proposals and quotations**

A Procurement Entity may reject any tender when the tenderer fails to meet a qualification in the predetermined or published requirement. The grounds for rejections shall be communicated to the Tenderers.

TEL: +233(0)548769918 /+233 (0) 501149296
Facebook Page: www.facebook.com/premiumicaglobal
Website: www.premiumonlinehub.com

> ➤ **Methods of Procurement**

1. Competitive Tendering:

This method of procurement is used by the Procurement Entity when it has the specific/formulate detailed speculations for the goods and gives all tenders equal opportunities.

2. Two – Stage Tendering:

This method is used when the Procurement Entity does not have specific specifications for the goods or services. The first stage gives tenderer opportunity to furnish the Procurement Entity with likely specifications which will meet the needs of the Procurement Entity and after that, the second stage is where each tenderer is given opportunity for bid for the contract.

- **First stage (Invitation Document)**
- **Second stage (Tender proceedings)**

3. Restricted Tendering

A Procurement Entity may for reasons of economy and efficiency and subject to the approval of the Board engage in procurement by means of Restricted Tendering.

Condition:

- If the goods, services or works are available from only limited number of suppliers or contractor.
- If the time and cost required to examine and evaluate a large number of tenders.

TEL: +233(0)548769918 /+233 (0) 501149296
Facebook Page: www.facebook.com/premiumicaglobal
Website: www.premiumonlinehub.com

4. **Single – Source Procurement**

A Procurement Entity may engaged in this method under section 41 with the approval of the Board.

Conditions:

- Where goods, works or service are only available from a particular supplier or contractor.
- Where there is an urgent need for the goods, works and services
- Where there is an additional requirement from a supplier or contractor who has supplied the Procurement Entity with goods, services or works.
- Where the Procurement Entity thinks in the best interest of National security a Single – Source Procurement method is used.

➢ **Tendering Procedures**

a. **National Competitive Tendering:**
   This is where the Procurement Entity decides that only domestic suppliers or contractors may submit tenderers.

b. **International Competitive Tendering:**
   This is where the Procurement Entity decides to allow foreign firms or tenderers to tender or bid for the contract.

➢ **Procedure for Inviting Tenders**

A Procurement Entity shall invite tenderers by publishing a document called Invitation to Tender in the newspaper. If it's an International Competitive Tendering, the document must also be published in at least one International newspapers.

TEL: +233(0)548769918 /+233 (0) 501149296
Facebook Page: www.facebook.com/premiumicaglobal
Website: www.premiumonlinehub.com

✓ **Contents of Invitation to Tender**
- Name and address of the Procurement Entity
- Specification of goods and place of delivery
- Time of delivery
- Criteria and procedure for evaluation
- Means of obtaining the Invitation of Document
- The price and currency as well as means of payment for the Invitation Document
- The place and deadlines for submission of Tenders
- The place, time and date for the opening of bids.

➢ **Clarification and Modification of Tender documents**

- A supplier may request promptly clarification of the tender documents from the Procurement Entity. The Procurement Entity shall within reasonable time before the deadline for the submission of Tender respond to the request.
- The Procurement Entity may modify the Invitation Document by issuing an addendum (textual matter added onto the publication) prior to the deadline for the submission of tender.

Examination of Tenders

The Procurement Entity may ask a supplier or contractor for clarification of its tender in order to assist in the examination, evaluation and comparison of tenders.

Evaluation of Tenders

- The Procurement Entity shall evaluate and ascertain the successful tender in accordance with the procedures and criteria set out in the Invitation Document.
- Upon choosing the successful tenderer, the necessary documents are assigned and come into effect.

TEL: +233(0)548769918 /+233 (0) 501149296
Facebook Page: www.facebook.com/premiumicaglobal
Website: www.premiumonlinehub.com

Methods and Procedures to Procure Consultants.

It follows the same procedures as under goods.

Review

- **Right to Review:**

  Any supplier that claims to have suffered any loss or injury due to a breach of a duty imposed on the Procurement Entity by this Act on;
  - The selection of a method of procurement
  - The choice of a selection procedure
  - The limitation of procurement proceedings
  - The decisions by the Procurement Entity.
  -

Review by Procurement Entity

A complaint shall in writing be submitted to the head of the Procurement Entity either before the or after the procurement contract comes into force. The Procurement Entity shall within 21 days after the submission of the complaint, issue a written decision concerning the complaint.

Administrative Review

If a supplier lodges complaints to the Procurement Entity and the Procurement Entity's response/decision doesn't suit the supplier, an official complaint is sent to the Public Procurement Authority (PPA).

- Upon the receipt of a complaint, the authority shall give notice of the complaint promptly to the Procurement Entity.

The decision by the Authority may be either;

- Declare the legal rules/principles that govern the subject – matter of the complaint

TEL: +233(0)548769918 /+233 (0) 501149296
Facebook Page: www.facebook.com/premiumicaglobal
Website: www.premiumonlinehub.com

- Annul in whole or in part an illegal act or decision of the Procurement Entity.
- Revise an illegal decision by the Procurement Entity or substitute its own decision for the decision of the Procurement Entity.
- Order that the procurement proceeding be terminated.

Disposal of stores, Plant and Equipment

a. Authority to dispose
- The head of a Procurement Entity shall convene a Board of Survey comprising representatives of departments with surplus, unserviceable and absolute stores and Plant & Equipment.
- The Board of Survey recommendations is approved by the head of the Procurement Entity as to how to dispose the stores.

b. Procedures for Disposal
- Transfer to government departments
- Sale by public tender to the highest tenderers
- Sale by public auction
- Destruction, dumping or burring as appropriate.

Procedures for Procurement at the District Assembly Level (Local Government)

- The storekeeper or head of spending units raises requisition by completing the Activity and Expenditure Initiation forms which is approved by the Heads of MDAs/MMDAs/Administration.
- Procurement Officer makes requests for quotation by inviting bids from potential surplus.
- Tender Committee reviews the bids and selects a supplier.

TEL: +233(0)548769918 /+233 (0) 501149296
Facebook Page: www.facebook.com/premiumicaglobal
Website: www.premiumonlinehub.com

- The Procurement Officer prepare the Purchase Order and sent to the Accountant to ensure that the transaction is properly charged and to commit the transaction against the Budget Allocation (Warrant) of the MMDAs.
- The accountant authorizes the Purchase Order and approve by the Head of the MDAs and MMDAs as a warrant
- The Purchase Order is sent to the supplier, goods is received and inspected by storekeeper and the Audit team.

TEL: +233(0)548769918 /+233 (0) 501149296
Facebook Page: www.facebook.com/premiumicaglobal
Website: www.premiumonlinehub.com

ACCOUNTABILITY AND VALUE FOR MONEY IN THE PUBLIC SECTOR

1.1. Introduction

ACCOUNTANILITY: The concept of accountability can be linked closely with the accountability both in the Private and Public Sector.

1.2. Accountability differences

1.2.1. **In PRIVATE SECTOR:** The owners/shareholders of the company employs a team of managers called Board of Directors who manages the company on behalf of the owners. The relationship is referred to as the **Agency Theory.** It then means that management take care of the company in the best interest of the shareholders. This is referred to as the **STEWARDSHIP** of management.

Management acting will have to be **ACCOUNTABLE** to shareholders on how best the resources committed under their stewardship have been managed. Management shows their Accountability through the **Financial Statements they** prepare.

1.2.2. **In PUBLIC SECTOR:** In the public sector, the citizenry vote the government into office and pay taxes that are then used by the Government to manage the country. Government then becomes the **STEWARD** of the public fund, and as such must be **ACCOUNTABLE** to the citizens of the country on how best the public funds have been utilised. It is only not about what the Government has done but also about **how much money (fund)** that was spent on what the Government has done.

With the Public Sector, the government is seen as **the actor or accounter** and the specific public is the **accountee.**

TEL: +233(0)548769918 /+233 (0) 501149296
Facebook Page: www.facebook.com/premiumicaglobal
Website: www.premiumonlinehub.com

1.3. THE FOUR ELEMENTS OF THE NOTION OF ACCOUNTABILITY

a. Public accessibility of the amount giving and not purely internal or discrete informing.
b. Explanation and justification of conduct and not propaganda
c. The explanation should be directed at a specific forum and not be given at a random.
d. The actor must feel obliged to come forward instead of being at liberty to provide any account whatsoever.

1.4. TYPES OF ACCOUNTABILITY RELATIONSHIP

In a democratic system such as Ghana, public managers face about five different sort of forums, with five different types of potential accountability relationship and five different sets of norms and expectation.

These are discussed as follows:

1. **Organisational Accountability:**

Public managers are accountable to their superior both administratively and politically. This is normally not to the entire citizenry.

2. **Political Accountability (Elected Representation):**

Public managers are accountable e.g. Ministers to appear before Parliament to account for the duties they have undertaken or perform during a given period of time.

3. **Legal Accountability (Courts, Committee or Commission of Enquiry):**

TEL: +233(0)548769918 /+233 (0) 501149296
Facebook Page: www.facebook.com/premiumicaglobal
Website: www.premiumonlinehub.com

Public managers can be summoned by courts, committee or commission of enquiry to account for their own acts or on behalf of the agency, department or ministry they head.

4. Administrative (Auditors, Inspectors and Controllers):

Public managers present accounts to the Auditor General for scrutiny for probing and legality of public spending as well as efficiency and effectiveness of their actions and/or their decision.

5. Professional Accountability (Professional Peers):

Some public managers also belong to professional bodies like the Institute of Chartered Accountants Ghana (ICA) and others. It means that these managers must be accountable for their action due to their membership to these bodies. Example; Public managers of hospitals, schools, psychiatric clinics, police departments or fire department.

1.5. THE ACCOUNTABILITY PROCESS

The government financial accountability process is divided into three stages:

1. Before the Financial Year:

The Government is required under the Constitution of the Republic of Ghana to present to Parliament for approval its proposed Budget which it needs to implement its policies and programmes. This is referred to as the **BUDGETING PROCESS.**

2. During the Financial Year:

To enable Parliament to maintain its Budgetary Control over the government, when the government needs to increase the Budget or levy new or higher taxes, it has to come back to Parliament for the approval of such decision. This is referred to as the **EXECUTION STAGE**

TEL: +233(0)548769918 /+233 (0) 501149296
Facebook Page: www.facebook.com/premiumicaglobal
Website: www.premiumonlinehub.com

3. **After the Financial Year:**

When the year ends, the government reports back to Parliament on its receipt and expenditure in a set of Government Financial Statements which are first subject to scrutiny by the Auditor -General who expresses an opinion on these statements. After which these statements are tabled before the **Public Accounts Committee** (which comprises of 25 Members of Parliament) **for closer examination.**

1.6. FOUR POSSIBLE MODELS OF ACCOUNTABILITY
1. Corporate Accountability :

Many Public organisations are seen as an independent legal entity which is responsible for its actions/decisions/policies. With this, each public organisation can be held accountable for any mishap or actions of the entity.

2. Hierarchical Accountability:

This is the most common model for accountability in that, the external accountability for the conduct of the organisation lies in the first instance wholly with the minister, the director or the commander in chief. With this, we can simply refer to an individual to be accountable for a ministry, a department or an organisation.

3. Collective Accountability:

Since public organisations are collective of individual officials, it means that any official can be accountable for the actions/policies/decisions of the organisation.

4. Individual Accountability:

With this model, each official is held liable in so far as and according to the extent to which he has personally contributed to the mal-performance of the public organisation/agency, irrespective of whether he is a junior official or the general manager.

TEL: +233(0)548769918 /+233 (0) 501149296
Facebook Page: www.facebook.com/premiumicaglobal
Website: www.premiumonlinehub.com

1.7. THE IMPORTANCE OF PUBLIC ACCOUNTABILITY

1. Democratic Control:

Since Ghana runs a Democratic system of Governance which requires citizens (voters), the Public Accountability Process provides both Political representatives and voters with the necessary inputs for judging the fairness, effectiveness, and efficiency of Governance.

2. Integrity:

The public character of the account giving is a safeguard against corruption, nepotism, abuse of power, and other forms of inappropriate behaviour. The assumption is that, public managers will be deterred from secretly misusing of power and public funds.

3. Improve performance:

When public managers are held accountable for their decisions/actions/policies year after year, they improve upon performance.

4. Legitimacy:

Accountability bridges the gap between citizens and representatives in the sense of transparency, responsiveness and answerability which enhances public confidence.

5. Catharsis:

Public officers/managers are released from the emotional tension from past behaviour since they account for everything they do on yearly basis.

TEL: +233(0)548769918 /+233 (0) 501149296
Facebook Page: www.facebook.com/premiumicaglobal
Website: www.premiumonlinehub.com

1.8. Summary

Functions	Dysfunctions
Democratic control	Rule- Obsession
Integrity	Proceduralism
Improvement	Rigidity
Legitimacy	Rising expectation
Catharsis	Scapegoating

2.1. VALUE FOR MONEY

2.2. Introduction

Value for Money describes an explicit commitment to ensuring the best results possible are obtained from the money spent.

Government uses Value for Money to reflect a concern for more transparency and accountability in spending public funds and for obtaining the maximum benefits from the resources available.

Donors and multilateral agencies like USAID, DANIDA, OECD, World Bank uses the concept of Value for money to appraise and evaluate the model of spending by government.

TEL: +233(0)548769918 /+233 (0) 501149296
Facebook Page: www.facebook.com/premiumicaglobal
Website: www.premiumonlinehub.com

2.3. Forms of Value for Money Assessment

1. **Auditing of Performance Management and Measurement Systems:**

This entails conducting regular audit of departmental systems, comparing actual with planned performance, trend analysis to make assessment for value for money.

2. **Economic Appraisal:**

This entails using an appraisal process to decide whether to invest in a proposed scheme or project.

2.4. KEY ELEMENTS OF VALUE FOR MONEY

"VFM is about obtaining the maximum benefit over time with the resources available. It is about achieving the right local balance between economy, efficiency and effectiveness, or spending less, spending well and spending wisely to achieve local priorities. …… VFM is high when there is an optimum balance between all three elements, when costs are relatively low, productivity is high and successful outcomes have been achieved"- UK Audit Commission

Value for money (VFM) is concerned with obtaining the best possible combination of services for the least resources. It is therefore the pursuit of
'Economy', 'Efficiency' and 'Effectiveness' – often referred to as the 3Es.

a. Economy – least cost. Accomplishes objectives and goals at a cost commensurate with the risk.
b. Efficiency – best use of resources. Accomplishes goals and objectives in an accurate and timely fashion with minimal use of resources.
c. Effectiveness – best results. Providing assurance that the organisation objectives will be achieved.

TEL: +233(0)548769918 /+233 (0) 501149296
Facebook Page: www.facebook.com/premiumicaglobal
Website: www.premiumonlinehub.com

Examples of local government indicators are given below:

• Economy – cost of waste collection per local taxpayer.
• Efficiency – number of households (premises) covered per waste collector.
• Effectiveness – % of waste recycled measured against target for the year.

2.5. The 4Cs

Best value is a requirement for local authorities to demonstrate achievement of the '4C' principles, as well as demonstrating service delivery and meeting customer needs through effective performance management systems.

• **Challenge** – review internally the different options for providing services and question the status quo.

• **Compare**– compare with other service providers to review options for improving performance.

• **Consult**– consult all users of services and those affected by services.

• **Compete**– demonstrate through performance management and continuous improvement that the most efficient and effective service is being provided.

2.6. CORPORATE GOVERNANCE PRINCIPLES FOR GOVERNING PUBLIC SECTOR ENTITIES.

The term "corporate governance" has no single accepted definition. It is generally understood to encompass how an organization is managed, its corporate and other structures, its culture, its policies and strategies, and the way in which it deals with its various stakeholders.

Public Sector Governance refers to the arrangements and practices which enable a public sector entity to set its direction and manage its operations

TEL: +233(0)548769918 /+233 (0) 501149296
Facebook Page: www.facebook.com/premiumicaglobal
Website: www.premiumonlinehub.com

to achieve expected outcomes and discharge its accountability obligations.

Public sector governance encompasses leadership, direction, control and accountability, and assists an entity, its decisions and its actions.

2.6.1. The objectives of Good Governance

Good governance generally focuses on two key requirements of public sector entities:

a. **Performance:** Governance arrangements and practices are designed and operate to shape the entity's overall results, including the successful delivery of government programs and services

b. **Accountability:** Governance arrangements and practices are designed and operate to provide visibility of results, to the entity's leadership, the government, the Parliament and the community and conform to applicable legislative and policy requirements as well as public expectations of openness, transparency and integrity.

2.6.2. The Legislative Framework

The legal framework for governance in Ghana which regulates the activities of Public entities is derived from the following sources:

- The 1992 Constitution
- The Financial Administration Act 2003 (Act 654)
- The Financial Administration Regulation 2004 (L.I. 1802)
- Public Services Commission Act 1994 (Act 482)

TEL: +233(0)548769918 /+233 (0) 501149296
Facebook Page: www.facebook.com/premiumicaglobal
Website: www.premiumonlinehub.com

2.6.3. Principles of Good Governance

In examining corporate governance literature, six main principles that public sector entities must adhere to in order to effectively apply the elements of corporate governance to achieve better practice governance can be identified.

Three of these elements (**leadership, integrity & commitment**) relate to **personal qualities** of those in the organization. The other three elements (**accountability, integration & transparency**) are mainly a product of **strategies, systems, policies & processes in place.**

Let's briefly discuss each of them

a. **Leadership:**
Effective public sector governance requires leadership from the governing Board and/or executive management of organizations. An effective framework requires clear identification and articulation of responsibility and a real understanding and appreciation of the various relationships between the organization's stakeholders and those who are entrusted to manage resources and deliver required outcomes.

b. **Commitment:**
Concern has been expressed that there has been more emphasis on the form rather than the substance of good corporate governance in both the public and private sectors in many countries.
It must be stressed that better practices public sector governance requires a strong commitment by all participants to effectively implement all elements of corporate governance.

c. **Integrity:**

Integrity is based on honesty and objectivity, as well as on high standards of propriety and probity in the stewardship of public funds and the management of an agency's affairs.

TEL: +233(0)548769918 /+233 (0) 501149296
Facebook Page: www.facebook.com/premiumicaglobal
Website: www.premiumonlinehub.com

d. **Accountability:**

In the public sector, the citizenry vote the government into office and pay taxes that are then used by the Government to manage the country. Government then becomes the **STEWARD** of the public fund, and as such must be **ACCOUNTABLE** to the citizens of the country on how best the public funds have been utilised. It is only not about what the Government has done but also about **how much money (fund)** that was spent on what the Government has done.

e. **Transparency:**

Openness or equivalent transparency is about providing stakeholder with complete confidence regarding the decision – making processes and actions of public sector agencies in managing their activities.

f. **Integration:**

The real challenge is not simply to define the various elements of effective corporate government but to ensure that they are holistically integrated into a coherent corporate approach by individual organizations and well understood and applied throughout those organizations.

2.7. Institutions and Structures that Ensures Public Accountability

The following institutions and structures are entrusted by the public financial management legislations to ensure public accountability.

1. The Auditor – General: Auditor General's report

The Auditor General is required to present his findings in a Report on the Public Accounts of' Ghana, which is submitted to Parliament.

The Auditor General's report is submitted to Parliament within six months. There are additional requirements in relation to the use and misuse of funds. His report must draw attention to any cases in which he has observed that:

- An officer or employee of Government has wilfully or negligently omitted to collect or receive any public money due to the Government

TEL: +233(0)548769918 /+233 (0) 501149296
Facebook Page: www.facebook.com/premiumicaglobal
Website: www.premiumonlinehub.com

- Any public money was not duly accounted for and paid into the Consolidated Fund or other designated public account
- An appropriation was exceeded or was applied for a purpose or in a manner not authorised by law
- An expenditure was not authorised or properly vouched for or certified
- There has been a deficiency through fraud, default or mistake of any person
- Applicable internal controls are inefficient or ineffective
- Resources have not been used with due regard to economy, efficiency and effectiveness in relation to the results attained
- In the public interest, the matter should be brought to the notice of Parliament

2. Public Accounts Committee of Parliament

The Public Accounts Committee (PAC) is one of the key accountability committees of Parliament.

The Public Accounts Committee (PAC) is one of 11 Standing Committees of the Parliament of Ghana as required by Article 103 of the Constitution of Ghana (1992).

It is established by Parliament Standing Order 151(2). The Committee, according to Standing Order 165(1), must consist of not more than 25 Members Id under the chairmanship of a member who does not belong to the party which controls the Executive branch of government. The composition of the Committee must as much as possible reflect the different shades of opinion in Parliament, as required by Article 103(5) of the constitution.

The PAC has the powers, rights and privileges of a High Court in relation to:

- Enforcing the attendance of witnesses and examining them on oath, affirmation or otherwise
- Compelling the production of documents

TEL: +233(0)548769918 /+233 (0) 501149296
Facebook Page: www.facebook.com/premiumicaglobal
Website: www.premiumonlinehub.com

- Issuing of a commission or requesting to examine witnesses abroad

The primary function of the PAC is to examine the audited accounts of government. It is Parliament which has exclusive powers in the financial management of the country. Through its PAC, therefore, Parliament is able to exercise control over the expenditure of monies which it manages.

3. Internal Audit Agency

The Internal Audit Agency aims to co-ordinate internal audit activities within public sector organisations in Ghana.

The Internal Audit Agency (IAA) was established by the Internal Audit Agency Act (2003). This was part of an overall move towards giving MDAs and MMDAs increased budgetary authority and expenditure control.

The IAA exists as an apex oversight body internal audit units working within MDAs and MMDAs. The Internal Audit Agency Act (2003) states that its object is to co-ordinate, facilitate and provide quality assurance for internal audit activities within the MDAs and the MMDAs.

2.7.1. Mission, values and objectives

The IAA's mission is:

'To exercise oversight responsibility over internal audit practice in the public service by coordinating, facilitating, and setting standards; providing quality assurance, and supporting capacity building for good corporate governance, and effective risk management.'

Its core guiding principles (values) are stated as: Integrity, Objectivity, Confidentiality and Professionalism.

TEL: +233(0)548769918 /+233 (0) 501149296
Facebook Page: www.facebook.com/premiumicaglobal
Website: www.premiumonlinehub.com

2.7.1.1. **The objectives of** the IAA are to:

- Contribute to the improvement of fair, transparent and accountable governance

- Re-brand internal audit practice in the public service of Ghana for improved visibility, public acceptability and support

It aims to achieve these by pursuing the following strategies:

- Improving Internal Audit Practice in MDAs/MMDAs
- Improving human resource capacity at the Agency for effective internal audit work
- Improving ICT capacity
- Strengthening Partnerships
- Training & Capacity Building for IAUs
- Sensitise the public for effective internal audit practice
- Convert the Agency into a Regulatory Authority

2.7.1.2. **Functions of the IAA**

The IAA is responsible for setting standards and procedures for the conduct of internal audit within MDAs and MMDAs. One way it has done this is by originating an internal audit manual written specifically for these audits.

The IAA is required to ensure that:

- Financial, managerial and operating information reported internally and externally is accurate, reliable and timely
- The financial activities of MDAs and MMDAs are in compliance with laws, policies, plans, standards and procedures
- National resources are adequately safeguarded
- National resources are used economically, effectively and efficiently

TEL: +233(0)548769918 /+233 (0) 501149296
Facebook Page: www.facebook.com/premiumicaglobal
Website: www.premiumonlinehub.com

- Plans, goals and objectives of MDAs and MMDAs are achieved
- Risks are adequately managed in the MDAs and MMDAs

Further, it must:

- Promote economy, efficiency and effectiveness in the administration of government programmes and operations
- Prepare plans to be approved by the Board for the development and maintenance of an efficient internal audit for the MDAs and MMDAs
- Facilitate the prevention and detection of fraud
- Provide a means for keeping the MDAs and MMDAs fully and currently informed about problems and deficiencies related to the administration of their programmes and operations and the necessity for appropriate corrective action

Finally, the IAA is required to monitor, undertake inspections and evaluate the internal auditing of the MDAs and MMDAs.

TEL: +233(0)548769918 /+233 (0) 501149296
Facebook Page: www.facebook.com/premiumicaglobal
Website: www.premiumonlinehub.com

GOVERNMENT BUDGETING AND BUDGETARY CONTROL

A. **LOCAL GOVERNMENT BUDGET AND FINANCIAL REPORTING SYSTEM**

1.1. Introduction

Structure and Levels of Governance of Local Government

Ghana has five levels of governance at the local level. They are made up of:

- Regional Coordinating Council
- Metropolitan Assembly
- Municipal / District Assembly
- Urban/ Town / Area / Zonal Councils
- Unit Committee

1.2. **The Local Government Act 462 1993** tells us how these are formed

(2) The President may by executive instrument –
a. declare any area within Ghana to be a district;
b. assign a name to the district

(3) The President shall in the exercise of his powers under sub-section (2)
(a) direct the Electoral Commission to make such recommendations as it considers appropriate for the purpose.

(4) The Electoral Commission shall before making recommendations to the President under sub-section (3) consider factors including –
     (a) in the case of –
          (i) a district that there is a minimum population of seventy-five thousand people;

          (ii) a municipal, that the geographical area consists of a single compact settlement and that there is a minimum of ninety – five thousand people;

TEL: +233(0)548769918 /+233 (0) 501149296
Facebook Page: www.facebook.com/premiumicaglobal
Website: www.premiumonlinehub.com

(iii) a metropolis, that there is a minimum of two hundred and fifty thousand people; and

(b) the geographical contiguity and economic viability of the areas

1.3. METROPOLITAN, MUNICIPAL AND DISTRICT ASSEMBLIES IN GHANA

Below is the structure of the MMDAs in Ghana as at 21st January 2017.

1. ASHANTI REGION

METROPOLITAN ASSEMBLIES	CAPITAL	L.I.
1. Kumasi	Kumasi	2059
MUNICIPAL ASSEMBLIES	**CAPITAL**	**L.I.**
2. Obuasi	Obuasi	
3. Ejisu-Juaben	Ejisu	1795
4. Bekwai	Bekwai	1890
5. Mampong	Mampong	1906
6. Offinso	Offinso	1908
7. Asokore Mampong	Asokore	1909
8. Asante Akim Central	Konongo-Odumase	2112
9. Ejura-Sekyidumase	Ejura	2056
		2098
DISTRICT ASSEMBLIES	**CAPITAL**	**L.I**
10. Ahafo-Ano South	Mankraso	1401
11. Ahafo-Ano North	Tepa	1402
12. Amansie West	Manso-Nkwanta	1403

TEL: +233(0)548769918 /+233 (0) 501149296
Facebook Page: www.facebook.com/premiumicaglobal
Website: www.premiumonlinehub.com

13. Asante-Akim South	Juaso	1409
14. Atwima Nwabiagya	Nkawie	1738
15. Adansi South	New Edubiase	1752
16. Adansi North	Fomena	
17. Amansie Central	Jacobu	1758
18. Atwima Mponua	Nyinahin	1774
19. Sekyere Central	Nsuta	1785
20. Bosome Freho	Asiwa	1841
21. Atwima Kwanwoma	Foase	1852
22. Offinso North	Akomadan	1853
23. Afigya-Kwabre	Kodie	1856
24. Kwabere East	Mamponteng	1856
25. Sekyere South	Agona	1894
26. Sekyere East	Effiduase	1898
27. Bosomtwe	Kuntanase	1900
28. Asante Akim North	Agogo	1922
29. Sekyere Afram Plains	Drobonso	2057
30. Sekyere Kumawu	Kumawu	2058
		2060
	TOTAL ASSEMBLIES	**30**

2. BRONG AHAFO REGION

MUNICIPAL ASSEMBLIES	CAPITAL	L.I.
1. Kintampo North	Kintampo	
2. Asunafo North	Goaso	1871
3. Berekum	Berekum	1873
4. Wenchi	Wenchi	1874
5. Sunyani	Sunyani	1876
6. Dormaa Central	Dormaa-Ahenkro	1924
7. Nkoranza South	Nkoranza	2087
8. Techiman		2089

TEL: +233(0)548769918 /+233 (0) 501149296
Facebook Page: www.facebook.com/premiumicaglobal
Website: www.premiumonlinehub.com

	Techiman	2096
DISTRICT ASSEMBLIES	**CAPITAL**	**L.I.**
9. Tano North		
10. Tano South	Duayaw Nkwanta	1754
11. Atebubu-Amantin	Bechem	1755
12. Asunafo South	Atebubu	1770
13. Jaman South	Kukoum	1773
14. Pru	Drobo	1777
15. Jaman North	Yeji	1778
16. Kintampo South	Sampa	1779
17. Nkoricua North	Jema	1781
18. Dormaa East	Busunya	1844
19. Sunyani West	Wamfie	1851
20. Asutifi South	Odumasi	1881
21. Sene West	Hwidiem	2054
22. Tain	Kwame Danso	2088
23. Sene East	Nsawkaw	2090
24. Banda	Kajaji	2091
25. Asutifi North	Banda Ahenkro	2092
26. Dormaa West	Kenyasi	2093
27. Techiman North	Nkran Nkwanta	2094
	Tuobodam	2095
	TOTAL ASSEMBLIES	**27**

TEL: +233(0)548769918 /+233 (0) 501149296
Facebook Page: www.facebook.com/premiumicaglobal
Website: www.premiumonlinehub.com

3. **CENTRAL REGION**

METROPOLITAN ASSEMBLIES	CAPITAL	L.I.
1. Cape Coast	Cape Coast	1927
MUNICIPAL ASSEMBLIES	CAPITAL	L.I.
2. Komenda-Edina Eguafo-Abirem	Elmina	
3. Assin North	Assin Foso	1857
4. Effutu	Winneba	1859
5. Upper Denkyira-East	Dunkwa-on-Offin	1860
6. Agona West	Swedru	1877
7. Awutu Senya East	Kasoa	1920
8. Mfantseman	Saltpond	2025
		2026
DISTRICT ASSEMBLIES	CAPITAL	L.I.
9. Asikuma-Odoben-Brakwa	Asikuma	1378
10. Abura-Asebu-Kwamankesse	Abura-Dunkwa	1381
11. Ajumako-Enyan-Essiam	Ajumako	1383
12. Assin South	Nsuaem-Kyekyewere	1760
13. Upper Denkyira-West	Diaso	1848
14. Gomoa East	Afransi	1883
	Apam	1896
15. Gomoa West	Nsaba	1921
16. Agona East		
17. Twifo Hemang Lower Denkyira	Hemang	2022
	Twifo Praso	2023
	Awutu-Breku	2024

TEL: +233(0)548769918 /+233 (0) 501149296
Facebook Page: www.facebook.com/premiumicaglobal
Website: www.premiumonlinehub.com

18. Twifo Ati-Morkwa 19. Awutu Senya 20. Ekumfi	Essarkyir	2027
	TOTAL ASSEMBLIES	**20**

4. EASTERN REGION

MUNICIPAL ASSEMBLIES	CAPITAL	L.I.
1. New-Juaben 2. Birim Central 3. Kwahu West 4. East Akim 5. Akwapim North 6. Lower ManyaKrobo 7. Nsawam Adoagyiri 8. Suhum 9. West Akim 10. YiloKrobo	Koforidua Akim-Oda Nkawkaw Kibi Akropong Akwapim Odumasi-Krobo Nsawam Suhum Asamankese Somanya	1426 1863 1870 1878 2041 2046 2047 2048 2050 2051
DISTRICT ASSEMBLIES	**CAPITAL**	**L.I**
11. Fanteakwah 12. Asuogyaman 13. Kwahu Sorth 14. Atiwa 15. Kwahu East 16. Upper Manya Krobo 17. Birim South 18. Akyemansa 19. Birim North	Begoro Atimpoku Mpraeso Kwabeng Abetifi Asesewa Akim Swedru Ofoase	1411 1431 1742 1784 1839 1842 1850 1919

TEL: +233(0)548769918 /+233 (0) 501149296
Facebook Page: www.facebook.com/premiumicaglobal
Website: www.premiumonlinehub.com

20. Akwapem South	New Abirem	1923
21. Denkyembour	Aburi	2040
22. Kwaebibirem	Akwatia	2042
23. Kwahu Afram Plains North	Kade	2043
	Donkorkrom	2044
24. Kwahu Afram Plains South	Tease	2045
	Adeiso	2049
25. Upper West Akim	Coaltar	2052
26. Ayensuano		
	TOTAL ASSEMBLIES	**26**

5.   GREATER ACCRA REGION

METROPOLITAN ASSEMBLIES	CAPITAL	L.I.
1. Accra		
2. Tema	Accra	2034
	Tema	2033
MUNICIPAL ASSEMBLIES	**CAPITAL**	**L.I.**
3. Ga West	Amasaman	1858
4. Ga East	Abokobi	1864
5. Ledzokuku-Krowor	Teshi-Nungua	1865
6. Adentan	Adentan	1888
7. Ashiaman	Ashiaman	1889
8. La Nkwantanang-Madina	Madina	2030
	Sowutuom	2036
9. Ga Central	Weija	2037
10. Ga South	La	2038
11. La Dede-Kotopon		

TEL: +233(0)548769918 /+233 (0) 501149296
Facebook Page: www.facebook.com/premiumicaglobal
Website: www.premiumonlinehub.com

DISTRICT ASSEMBLIES	CAPITAL	L.I.
12. Ada West 13. Ada East 14. Kpone Katamanso 15. Ningo Prampram 16. Shai-Osudoku	Sege Ada-Foah Kpone Prampram Dodowa	2028 2029 2031 2035 2039
	TOTAL ASSEMBLIES	**16**

6. NORTHERN REGION

METROPOLITAN ASSEMBLIES	CAPITAL	L.I.
1. Tamale	Tamale	2068
MUNICIPAL ASSEMBLIES	**CAPITAL**	**L.I.**
2. Yendi 3. Savelugu-Nanton	Yendi Savelugu	2070 2071
DISTRICT ASSEMBLIES	**CAPITAL**	**L.I.**
4. Bunkpurugu-Yunyoo 5. Central Gonja 6. Nanumba North 7. Nanumba South 8. Sawla Tuna Kalba 9. East Mamprusi	Bunkpurugu Buipe Bimbilla Wulensi Sawla	1748 1750 1754 1763 1768

TEL: +233(0)548769918 /+233 (0) 501149296
Facebook Page: www.facebook.com/premiumicaglobal
Website: www.premiumonlinehub.com

10. Gushiegu	Gambaga	1776
11. Bole	Gushiegu	1783
12. Karaga	Bole	1786
	Karaga	1787
13. Kpandai		
14. Chereponi		
15. Saboba		
16. East Gonja	Kpandai	1845
17. Zabzugu	Chereponi	1854
18. West Mamprusi	Saboba	1904
19. Kumbugu	Salaga	1938
20. Mambrugu	Zabzugu	2053
Moagduri	Walewale	2061
21. Mion	Kumbugu	2062
22. North Gonja	Yagaba	2063
23. Sagnerigu	Sang	2064
24. Tatale Sanguli	Daboya	2065
25. West Gonja	Sagnerigu	2066
26. Tolon	Tatale	2067
	Damongo	2069
	Tolon	2142
	TOTAL ASSEMBLIES	**26**

7. UPPER EAST REGION

MUNICIPAL ASSEMBLIES	CAPITAL	L.I.
1. Bolgatanga		1797
2. Bawku	Bolgatanga	2103
3. Kassenu / Nankana	Bawku	2106
	Navrongo	
DISTRICT ASSEMBLIES	**CAPITAL**	**L.I.**
4. Bawku-West		
5. Bongo	Zebilla	1442

TEL: +233(0)548769918 /+233 (0) 501149296
Facebook Page: www.facebook.com/premiumicaglobal
Website: www.premiumonlinehub.com

6. Garu-Tempane	Bongo	1446
7. Kassena/Nankana West	Garu	1769
	Paga	1895
8. Builsa South	Fumbisi	2104
9. Nabdam	Nangodi	2105
10. Binduri	Binduri	2107
11. Pusiga	Pusiga	2108
12. Talensi	Tongo	2110
13. Builsa North	Sandema	2148
	TOTAL ASSEMBLIES	**13**

8. UPPER WEST REGION

MUNICIPAL ASSEMBLIES	CAPITAL	L.I.
1. Wa	Wa	1800

DISTRICT ASSEMBLIES	CAPITAL	L.I.
2. Wa East		
3. Wa West	Funsi	1746
4. Sissala East	Weichiau	1751
5. Sissala West	Tumu	1766
6. Lambussie / Kani	Gwollu	1771
7. Jirapa	Lambussie	1849
8. Daffiama-Bussie-Issa	Jirapa	1902
9. Nadowli-Kaleo	Issa	2100
10. Nandom	Nadowli	2101
11. Lawra	Nandom	2102
	Lawra	2099

TEL: +233(0)548769918 /+233 (0) 501149296
Facebook Page: www.facebook.com/premiumicaglobal
Website: www.premiumonlinehub.com

	TOTAL ASSEMBLIES	11

9. VOLTA REGION

MUNICIPAL ASSEMBLIES	CAPITAL	L.I.
1. Keta	Keta	1868
2. Hohoe	Hohoe	2072
3. Kpando	Kpando	2073
4. Ho	Ho	2074
5. Ketu South	Denu	2155

DISTRICT ASSEMBLIES	CAPITAL	L.I.
6. Kadjebi		
7. South Tongu	Kadjebi	1465
8. South Dayi	Sogakope	1466
9. Krachi East	Kpeve	1753
10. Nkwanta North	Dambai	1755
11. Biakoye	Kpasa	1846
12. Nkwanta South	Nkonya-Ahenkro	1887
13. Ketu North	Nkwanta	1892
14. Jasikan	Dzodze	1897
15. North Dayi	Jasikan	1901
16. Central Tongu	Amfoegu	2076
17. Krachi West	Adidome	2077
18. Afadzato-South	Kete-Krachi	2078
19. Agortime Ziope	Ve-Golokwati	2079
	Agortime-Kpetoe	2080
20. North Tongu		
21. Akatsi North		
22. Ho West		
23. Krachi Ntsumuru	Battor Dugame	2081
24. Adaklu	Ave Dakpa	2082
25. Akatsi South	Dzolokpuita	2083
	Chinderi	2084

TEL: +233(0)548769918 /+233 (0) 501149296
Facebook Page: www.facebook.com/premiumicaglobal
Website: www.premiumonlinehub.com

	Adaklu Waya	2085
	Akatsi	2086
	TOTAL ASSEMBLIES	**25**

10. WESTERN REGION

METROPOLITAN ASSEMBLIES	CAPITAL	L.I.
1. Sekondi-Takoradi	Sekondi	1928
MUNICIPAL ASSEMBLIES	**CAPITAL**	**L.I.**
2. Tarkwa-Nsueman	Tarkwa	1886
3. Nzema East	Axim	1917
4. Sefwi Wiaso	Sefwi Wiaso	2015
DISTRICT ASSEMBLIES	**CAPITAL**	**L.I.**
5. Bibiani-Anhwiaso Bekwai	Bibiani	1387
6. Jomoro	Half-Assini	1394
7. Ahanta West	Agona Nkwanta	1395
8. Amenfi West	Wassa Akropong	1757
9. Prestea-Huni Valley	Bogoso	1840
10. Shama	Shama	1882
11. Sefwi Akontombra	Sefwi Akontombra	1884
12. Ellembelle	Nkroful	1918
13. Wassa Amenfi Central	Manso Amenfi	2011
14. Wassa Amenfi West	Asankragua	2012
15. Bia West	Essam-Dabiso	2013
16. Bia East	Adabokrom	2014
17. Suaman	Dadieso	2016
18. Aowin	Enchi	2017
19. Wassa East	Daboase	2018
	Mpohor	2019

TEL: +233(0)548769918 /+233 (0) 501149296
Facebook Page: www.facebook.com/premiumicaglobal
Website: www.premiumonlinehub.com

20. Mpohor 21. Juaboso 22. Bodie	Juabeso Bodie	2020 2021
	TOTAL ASSEMBLIES	**22**

1.3.1. SUMMARY OF STRUCTURE

REGIONS	MMDAs	CONSTITUENCIES
Ashanti Region	30	39
Brong Ahafo Region	27	24
Central Region	20	19
Eastern Region	26	28
Greater Accra Region	16	27
Northern Region	26	26
Upper East Region	13	13
Upper West Region	11	10
Volta Region	25	22
Western Region	22	22

Metropolitan Assemblies	6
Municipal Assemblies	56
District Assemblies	154
Total MMDAs	**216**
Number of Constituencies	275

PURPOSE: Bringing Local Governance to the Doorsteps of the People, and Enhance Decentralization Process in Ghana.

The present local government system in Ghana was established in 1988 by the military administration of Jerry Rawlings and the Provisional National Defense Council (PNDC). It is multi-tiered and at present comprises ten Regional Coordinating Councils under which are six Metropolitan Assemblies, fifty – six Municipal Assemblies and one hundred and twenty-four District Assemblies.

TEL: +233(0)548769918 /+233 (0) 501149296
Facebook Page: www.facebook.com/premiumicaglobal
Website: www.premiumonlinehub.com

1.4. THE LOCAL GOVERNMENT SERVICE

THE SIX HUNDRED AND FIFTY-SIXTH ACT OF THE PARLIAMENT OF THE REPUBLIC OF GHANA ENTITLED
THE LOCAL GOVERNMENT SERVICE ACT, 2003

AN ACT to establish a Local Government Service and to provide for the objects, functions, administration and management of the Service and for connected purposes.

1.4.1. Membership of the Service

2. The Service shall comprise persons holding non-elected public office in

(a) Regional Co-ordinating Councils;

(b) District Assemblies;

(c) Sub-Metropolitan District Councils, Urban, Zonal, Town and Area Councils;

(d) the Secretariat of the Service; and

(e) such other persons as may be employed for the Service.

1.4.2. Object of the Service

3. The object of the Service is to secure the effective administration and management of local government in the country.

1.4.3. Functions of the Service

4. (1) For the purpose of achieving its object, the Service shall

(a) provide technical assistance to District Assemblies, and Regional Coordinating
Councils to enable the District Assemblies and the Regional Coordinating Councils effectively perform their functions and discharge their duties in accordance with the Constitution and the Local Government Act,

TEL: +233(0)548769918 /+233 (0) 501149296
Facebook Page: www.facebook.com/premiumicaglobal
Website: www.premiumonlinehub.com

1993 (Act 462);

(b) conduct organisational and job analysis for the Regional Co-ordinating Councils and the District Assemblies;

(c) conduct management audits for Regional Co-ordinating Councils and District Assemblies in order to improve the overall management of the Service;

(d) design and co-ordinate management systems and processes for Regional
Co-ordinating Councils and District Assemblies;

(e) assist the Regional Co-ordinating Councils and the District Assemblies in the performance of their functions under the Local Government Act, 1993,
(Act 462), the National Development Planning (Systems) Act, 1994, (Act 480) and under any other enactment;

(f) perform such other functions incidental or conducive to the achievement of the objects of this Act.

1.4.4.   Governing body of the Service

5. (1) The governing body for the Service shall be known as the Local Government
Service Council referred to in this Act as "the Council".

(2) The Council shall consist of

(a) a chairperson who shall be a person with extensive experience in local government matters;

(b) a representative of the Ministry responsible for Local Government other than the Minister or the Deputy Minister;

(c) a representative of the National Development Planning Commission;

TEL: +233(0)548769918 /+233 (0) 501149296
Facebook Page: www.facebook.com/premiumicaglobal
Website: www.premiumonlinehub.com

(d) a representative of the Ghana Education Service;

(e) a representative of the Ghana Health Service;

(f) the Head of the Service;

(g) the Administrator of the District Assemblies Common Fund or a representative of the Administrator;

(h) a representative of the National Association of Local Authorities of Ghana
(NALAG);

(i) a representative of the Local Government Workers' Union;

(j) a representative of the Institute of Local Government Studies;

(k) a representative of the National House of Chiefs; and

(l) four other persons with considerable knowledge of local government matters at least two of whom are women.

(3) The chairperson and other members of the Council shall be appointed by the President in consultation with the Council of State.

1.4.5. Functions of the Council

6. The Council shall have general management and control of the Service and shall

(a) recommend to the Minister matters of policy relating to the management of the Service;

(b) ensure the implementation of the functions of the Service;

TEL: +233(0)548769918 /+233 (0) 501149296
Facebook Page: www.facebook.com/premiumicaglobal
Website: www.premiumonlinehub.com

(c) recommend to the Minister a scheme of service prescribing the terms and conditions of service as well as the remuneration of the employees of the
Service;

(d) develop policy guidelines for handling matters relating to recruitment, training, promotion, remuneration, discipline, arbitration and petition within the Service;

(e) set performance standards within which District Assemblies and Regional
Co-ordinating Councils shall carry out their functions and discharge their duties;

(f) monitor and evaluate the performance standards of District Assemblies and
Regional Co-ordinating Councils;

(g) develop and co-ordinate the personnel plans and assess the personnel needs of the District Assemblies and the Regional Co-ordinating Councils in consultation with the respective Assemblies and Co-ordinating Councils;

(h) develop and co-ordinate the training implementation plans of District Assemblies and Regional Co-ordinating Councils in consultation with the respective Assemblies and Co-ordinating Councils;

(i) develop professional standards and guidelines for the various categories of staff who are members of the Service;

(j) work in consultation and close co-operation with other services of the public service;

(k) perform such other functions as may be assigned to it by or under this Act or any other enactment; and

(l) advise the Minister on such matters as the Minister may request.

TEL: +233(0)548769918 /+233 (0) 501149296
Facebook Page: www.facebook.com/premiumicaglobal
Website: www.premiumonlinehub.com

1.5. Office of the Regional Co-ordinating Council

16. (1) There shall be an office of the Regional Co-ordinating Council in each region of the country.

(2) The Regional Co-ordinating Director shall be the administrative head of the
Regional Co-ordinating Council and shall be responsible to the Regional Minister.

(3) The Regional Co-ordinating Director shall have the conditions of service as may be determined by the Council.

(4) The Regional Co-ordinating Director shall ensure the effective and efficient performance of the office of the Regional Co-ordinating Council.

(5) A person assigned from any public office to the office of the Regional Coordinating
Council shall be an officer of the Regional Co-ordinating Council.

(6) The Regional Co-ordinating Council shall be responsible for the work, career progression and discipline of the officers of the Regional Co-ordinating Council.

1.5.1. Departments of the Regional Co-ordinating Council

17. (1) Government departments in any region of the Civil Service shall be known as Departments of the Regional Co-ordinating Council.

(2) The heads of departments of a Regional Co-ordinating Council are answerable in the performance of their duties to the Regional Co-ordinating Council.

TEL: +233(0)548769918 /+233 (0) 501149296
Facebook Page: www.facebook.com/premiumicaglobal
Website: www.premiumonlinehub.com

1.5.1.1. Functions of Departments of Regional Co-ordinating Council

18. The Departments of a Regional Co-ordinating Council shall

(a) implement the decisions of the Regional Co-ordinating Council; and

(b) provide quarterly reports on the implementation of policies and programmes to the Regional Co-ordinating Council through the office of the Regional Co-ordinating Council.

1.6. Functions of Departments of District Assembly

24. The Departments of District Assemblies shall

(a) be responsible for the implementation of the decisions of the District Assemblies; and

(b) provide quarterly reports on the implementation of decisions of the Assemblies to the Executive Committees of the respective District Assemblies through the offices of the District Assembly.

1.7. PART III—FINANCIAL PROVISIONS

1. Expenses of the Service

28. The expenses of the Service, including the administrative expenses, salaries, allowances, operational and other expenses of the Service, as well as retirement benefits payable in respect of persons employed by the Service, shall be a charge on the Consolidated Fund.

2. Submission of budget estimates

29. (1) The Head of Service shall, not later than three months before the end of each financial year, prepare and submit to the Minister through the Council, the budget estimates of expenditure to be incurred by the Service during the next financial year.

TEL: +233(0)548769918 /+233 (0) 501149296
Facebook Page: www.facebook.com/premiumicaglobal
Website: www.premiumonlinehub.com

(2) The budget estimates shall be in the form approved for that purpose by the Minister responsible for Finance.

(3) New or special expenditure shall receive the approval of the Council before being submitted to the Minister for approval.

(4) Except with the approval of the Minister responsible for Finance, given in consultation with the Minister, no further sum shall be expended during a financial year other than as provided in the estimates relating to the financial year.

3. Accounts and audit

30. (1) The Service shall keep books of account and proper records in relation to them which shall be prepared in a form approved by the Auditor-General.

(2) The Auditor-General shall audit the accounts of the Service within six months after the end of each financial year.

(3) The financial year of the Service shall be the same as the financial year of the government.

4. Annual report and other reports

31. (1) The Council shall within eight months after the end of each financial year submit to the Minister an annual report covering the activities and the operations of the Service for the year to which the report relates.

(2) The annual report submitted under subsection (1) shall include the report of the Auditor-General.

(3) The Council shall also submit to the Minister such other reports as the Minister may require in writing.

TEL: +233(0)548769918 /+233 (0) 501149296
Facebook Page: www.facebook.com/premiumicaglobal
Website: www.premiumonlinehub.com

(4) The Minister shall within two months after the receipt of the annual report submit a report to Parliament with such statement as the Minister may consider necessary.

1.8. Financial Relations between Central and Local Government

There are a number of legal rules and regulations which govern the financial relations of central government with local authorities.

1.8.1. **One set of rules involve financial arrangements for raising funds. They include**:

a. Tapping of own revenue (Act 245 and 252 of 1992) Constitution and Section 34, Part VII, VIII, IX and X of act 462 ;

b. Institution of Ceded Revenue Sixth Schedule of Act 462

c. Establishment of District Assembly Common Fund Act (Act 455)

d. Other specialized funding arrangements including Stool Lands, Royalties, Timber, Minerals Development Funding, Revenue from Lotto Operators and special payments by agencies and companies operating in the area of jurisdiction District Assemblies.

e. Recurrent Expenditure Transfers

1.8.2. **A second set of rules are meant to ensure transparency, accountability and efficiency, in the management of finances of Local authorities**:

a. Merger of central and local government treasuries at the district level into one District Finance Office;

b. Decentralization of the award and payment for contracts up to limits set by the Ministry of Finance;

c. Establishment of District Tender Boards under L.I 1606 (1995)

d. Act 462 section 91 of power of the Minister for Local Government to give financial instructions to District Assemblies;

TEL: +233(0)548769918 /+233 (0) 501149296
Facebook Page: www.facebook.com/premiumicaglobal
Website: www.premiumonlinehub.com

e. Section 93 (1) power of the Minister of Local Government to authorize the inspection of books, accounts and records of District Assemblies;

f. Act 462 section 92(1) Every District shall before the end of each financial year, submit to the Regional Coordinating Council a detailed budget for the district stating the revenue and expenditure of the District for the year

g. The Regional Coordinating Council shall collate and co-ordinate the budget of the districts in the region and shall submit the total budget to the Minister responsible for Finance and submit copies to the Regional Minister and the National Development Planning Committee;

h. The budget for a district shall include the aggregate revenue and expenditure of all departments and organizations under the District Assembly and the District Co-ordinating Directorate, including the annual development plans and programmes of the departments and organizations under the Assembly.

i. Every District Assembly should produce annual statement of accounts. The Auditor General is expected to produce his report; and the Auditor General shall publish his reports on Public accounts and present them to the Speaker to be laid before Parliament.

1.9. The Common Fund

The Common Fund under Act 455 of 1993 is defined as "a fund consisting of all monies allocated by parliament and any interest and dividends accruing from investments of monies from the common fund".

Functions of the District Assembly Common Fund Administrator

a. Propose a formula annually for the distribution of the common fund for approval by parliament.
b. To administer and distribute monies paid into the common fund among the district Assemblies in accordance with the formula approved by Parliament.

TEL: +233(0)548769918 /+233 (0) 501149296
Facebook Page: www.facebook.com/premiumicaglobal
Website: www.premiumonlinehub.com

c. To report in writing to the minister of Finance on how allocations made from the funds have been utilized by the District Assemblies.

d. To perform any other functions that may be directed by the President.

1.9.1. ALLOCATION OF THE FUND

Since the District Assemblies Common Fund

In accordance with Section 9 of the DACF Act 1993, Act 455, the following Guidelines for Utilisation of the DACF by Assemblies are used. This is in collaboration with the Ministry of Finance and in accordance with the decision of Cabinet.

1. Reserve Fund

Fifteen percent (15%) will be retained as a reserve Fund and used as follows:

a. Six percent of the Reserve Fund (that is 6% of the total DACF allocation for the year)

b. 1.5 % is allocated to the ten Regional Coordinating Council to be used for their statutory role of monitoring, Coordinating and evaluation of the performance of Assemblies. The allocation of this portion is as follows: 50% is shared equally to the ten regions and the remaining 50% in proportion to the number of district in the Region.

c. 2 % to be used as reserves under the discretion of the Minister

d. 0.5% to be used by DACF Administrator for monitoring and Evaluation

e. 5.0% to be used as contribution towards District Development facility and sanitation program.

TEL: +233(0)548769918 /+233 (0) 501149296
Facebook Page: www.facebook.com/premiumicaglobal
Website: www.premiumonlinehub.com

Of the remaining share, the following allocations should be made by each assembly:

a. **Human Capacity Building:**

One percent (1%) of each District Assembly share of the DACF will be deducted to finance the cost of training and other capacity building program for Assemblies. This item should be included in the DACF Budget of all Assemblies.

b. **National Youth Employment Programme:**

35% will be utilized to set up a fund for the purpose of Youth Employment Programme. Activities selected to benefit from this fund should be in conformity with the poverty profiles of the District and with the Ghana Poverty Reduction Strategy (GPRS). The NYEP under Common Fund will be utilized for Sanitation activities.

c. **District Response Initiative:**

Half percent (0.5%) may be utilized to support the District Response Initiative on HIV/AIDS

d. **Malaria Prevention (0.5%)**

e. **People with Disabilities (2%) :** This Fund is meant to assist people with disabilities to organize programmes to create awareness about their activities, their rights and obligations, among others.

f. **Other projects:**

The remaining sixty –one percent (61%) may be used in the following areas:

- Economic ventures: energy, roads, streets, private sector support, etc.

- Social services: education, health, water supply, etc.

TEL: +233(0)548769918 /+233 (0) 501149296
Facebook Page: www.facebook.com/premiumicaglobal
Website: www.premiumonlinehub.com

- Administration: human resource management, accommodation, other facilities, etc.

- Environment: sanitation, drainage system, waste management and environment protection.

1.9.2. District Assembly Common Fund (DACF) GUIDELINES

Guidelines for the Utilisation of 60% of the Reserve Fund Allocated to Parliamentary Constituencies

1. **Allocation of parliamentary Constituencies:**

In approving the formula for sharing the DACF, Parliament by a consensus decision in 1997, resolved that 60% of the 10% DACF allocation to the Reserve Fund be shared on Parliamentary Constituency basis and that the utilisation of this amount should be for projects selected and approved by the Members of Parliament.

The following revised instructions are provided in accordance with this allocation:

- The amount shall be shared equally among the 275 Parliamentary Constituencies

- The amount shall be released quarterly to the assemblies by the Administrator of the DACF and the Member of Parliament shall be notified

- A separate account shall be kept in respect of every constituency.

- Under no circumstance shall money be withdrawn from this account without a memorandum from the sitting Member of Parliament from that Constituency

- Where a memorandum has been raised to the District Chief Executive (DCE) for a project to be financed under this fund, the Member of Parliament shall be given a reply within fourteen working days as to whether the request has been passed or whether query has been raised.

- Payment from the account shall be made by the Finance Officer of the Assembly.

TEL: +233(0)548769918 /+233 (0) 501149296
Facebook Page: www.facebook.com/premiumicaglobal
Website: www.premiumonlinehub.com

- Accounting for this fund shall form part of the accounts of the Assembly and shall be incorporated in the financial returns of the Assembly.

- The DCE shall submit half –yearly progress on the operation of the constituency account to the Member of Parliament with copies to: the Presiding Member for the information of the Assembly.

- The Regional Minister shall compile the district-half yearly returns into the Regional returns and transmit to the Minister for Local Government and Rural Development.

2. **Guidelines for selection of Projects**

The selection of projects for support by the Member of Parliament under the Constituency Fund should conform to National and District Specific Development plans and objectives and should;

a. Fall within the scope of functions of District Assemblies

b. Correspond to the poverty reduction strategy of the Assembly

c. Provide infrastructure in the areas of education, health, agriculture, water, sanitation, roads, streets and drains.

d. Generate sustainable employment

e. Aim at income generation and wealth

f. Assist in disaster prevention and disaster relief.

3. **Joint Project with the Sector Minister**

Projects which fall within the functions of sector Ministries such as clinics under health, and school buildings under Education which will require additional input to become operational or future repairs and maintenance, should have the approval of the relevant sector Ministry.

TEL: +233(0)548769918 /+233 (0) 501149296
Facebook Page: www.facebook.com/premiumicaglobal
Website: www.premiumonlinehub.com

2.0. FINANCIAL ACCOUNTING AND BUDGETARY CONTROL

1. **Development of Budget**

    The Budget Development process at the Local Government Level takes the following steps or procedures:

    a. Each Assembly shall each year prepare a Development Budget covering the DACF. This is because, allocation of the DACF are not made before the commencement of the District Assembly's financial year of January to December.

    b. The Development Budget shall be presented in the approved form and shall be approved by a Resolution of the Assembly in accordance with the Local Government Act, 462 and transmitted along with a copy of the resolution to the Regional Coordinating Council.

    c. The Regional Co-ordinating Council will collate and harmonise Development Budgets approved by Assemblies into a Regional District Assembly Common Fund Budget. However, the RCC must ensure that projects, programmes and other activities in the District Assemblies' Budget are in conformity with the Ghana Poverty Reduction Strategy.

    d. The RCC shall distribute the collated Regional District Assemblies Common Fund Budget to:

    *   The Administrator of the District Assemblies Common Fund;

    *   The Ministry of Local Government and Rural Development;

    *   The Ministry of Finance;

    *   The National Development Planning Commission.

TEL: +233(0)548769918 /+233 (0) 501149296
Facebook Page: www.facebook.com/premiumicaglobal
Website: www.premiumonlinehub.com

2. **Stages in the preparation and approval of Metropolitan, Municipal and District Assemblies (MMDA's) Budget:**

Stages of Budget Preparation

a. Formation of a Budget Committee

b. Budget forms are designed and circulated.

c. Budget forms are filled by various budget Centres

d. Heads of Budget Units are called to defend their budget proposals.

e. Departmental budgets are collated into one budget.

f. Draft budgets are submitted to the Executive Committee

g. Executive Committee examines the budget and propose changes if necessary

h. The Assembly meets and approves the Budget.

3. **Accounting for Utilisation of the Fund:**

Financial Reports indicating:

a. Amount utilized;

b. Balance in the District Assembly Common Fund Account;

c. Outstanding contractual financial commitment for the succeeding period of three months should be submitted by the District Assembly at the end of each quarter (that is end of March, June, September and December) into the prescribe form and distributed to:

- The Administrator of the District Assemblies Common Fund;

- The Ministry of Local Government and Rural Development;

- The Ministry of Finance;

- RCC;

- The Member (s) of Parliament from the District.

- The Controller and Accountant General;

TEL: +233(0)548769918 /+233 (0) 501149296
Facebook Page: www.facebook.com/premiumicaglobal
Website: www.premiumonlinehub.com

2.1. Monthly Trial Balance, Receipt & Payments Statement, and Bank Reconciliation Statement

The periodic receipts from the DACF and expenditure therefore should be incorporated in the monthly trial balance in two forms.

a.   Project by project recorded expenditure

b.   All requested payments of the Administrator of the DACF on behalf of Assemblies should be recorded in the relevant books of Accounts of the Assemblies and reflected in the Trial balance, receipt and payment, reconciliation statements and other financial reports.

c.   Any unspent balance of the Assembly's share of the DACF should under no circumstance be **credited to the Accumulated Surplus Fund** of the Assembly. This balance should be treated as part of finances of net assets in the balance sheet.

4.   Projects Implementation & Reporting

5.   Award of Contract

6.   Payment from the DACF

7.   Supervision and Monitoring of Projects by RCC

8.   Disbursement on basis of Zonal, Urban, Town and Area Council.

TEL: +233(0)548769918 /+233 (0) 501149296
Facebook Page: www.facebook.com/premiumicaglobal
Website: www.premiumonlinehub.com

B. OVERVIEW OF BUDGETING BY CENTRAL GOVERNMENT

1.1. Introduction

The local authorities in Ghana still use the **Incremental line – item budgeting system** different from the **Medium – Term Expenditure Framework (**MTEF) budgeting system of the Central Government. There is normally a review of past year's outturn against the budget which marks the beginning of budget preparation. The budget actual of the year to date are compared to the budgeted figures of the variances are established.

A distinction is also made between committed and uncommitted items and resources.

1.2. Concept of Budgeting

The revised budget format of the Financial Memoranda for District Assemblies is designed with an accumulated surplus. This gives the impression that the concept of budgeting envisaged for local authorities is one of a surplus budget or perhaps a balanced budget on the assumption that projections do not show the normal growth pattern of revenue and expenditure.

1.3. Structure, Content and Format of Local Government Budget

The revised Financial Memoranda of District Assemblies explain the structure, content and format of the MMDA budget. It must however be emphasized that although the MMDA prepare, execute and evaluate their own budget, the Minister of Local Government may make an input, especially in the development budget.

Again, because the budget is structured on line- item incremental bases, budget objectives, programmes and plans are not easily discernible, simply by looking at the presentational format.

A Budget is an authorized financial plan of the anticipated revenues and expenditures of the government.

A budget deficit is a type of budget where the estimated expenditure exceeds the estimated revenues

TEL: +233(0)548769918 /+233 (0) 501149296
Facebook Page: www.facebook.com/premiumicaglobal
Website: www.premiumonlinehub.com

1.4. Uses of Budget:

- As a guide for the present and future
- To plan, control and estimate the amount to be received and spent during a specific period
- To distribute limited resources
- To motivate managers towards the achievement of corporate goals
- As a means of evaluating performance

1.5. Objectives of a Budgetary Control System

1. Authorisation

A budget may act as a formal authorisation to a manager to spend a given amount on specified activities. If this is applied to an operating budget, however, it must be appreciated that over-strict enforcement would not be in the best interest of the business.

2. Forecasting

Forecasting refers to the prediction of events over which little or no control is exercised. Some parts of all budgets are, therefore, based on forecast. Budget figures may also be used by one part of an organization to forecast the likely impact on the activities of other parts.

3. Planning

Planning is an attempt to shape the future by a conscious attempt to affect those factors, which are open to influence and control.

4. Control

A budget enhances management's ability of manage "by exception". Management attention is drawn to areas, which do not meet budget.

TEL: +233(0)548769918 /+233 (0) 501149296
Facebook Page: www.facebook.com/premiumicaglobal
Website: www.premiumonlinehub.com

5. Communications and Co-ordination

Budgets communicate plans to managers responsible for carrying them out. They also ensure co-ordination between managers of sub-units so that each is aware of the others" requirements.

6. Motivation

Budgets are often intended to motivate managers to work to a target (i.e. in line with organizational objectives).

7. Evaluation

The performance of mangers and organizational units is often evaluated by reference to budgetary standard (which may be the only quantitative reference points available). The way in which performance is evaluated will influence how a manager behaves in the future.

1.6. Guideline for Revenue and Expenditure Estimates

The Financial Administration Act, (Act 654) 2003,
PART III—REVENUE AND EXPENDITURE

Estimates of revenue and expenditure

25. (1) Subject to Article 179 of the Constitution, the President shall cause to be prepared and laid before Parliament at least one month before the end of the financial year, estimates of the revenues and expenditure of the Government for the following financial year.

(2) The estimates of the expenditure of departments and agencies

(a) shall be classified under programmes or activities which shall be included in a Bill to be known as the Appropriation Bill and which shall be introduced into Parliament to provide for the issue from the Consolidated Fund or such other appropriate fund of the sums of money necessary to meet that expenditure and the appropriation of those sums for the purposes specified in that Bill;

TEL: +233(0)548769918 /+233 (0) 501149296
Facebook Page: www.facebook.com/premiumicaglobal
Website: www.premiumonlinehub.com

(b) shall outline for each vote of expenditure a statement of the performance criteria to be met in providing the required outputs; and

(c) shall in respect of payments charged on the Consolidated Fund, be laid before Parliament for the information of Members of Parliament.

(3) Parliament shall determine the procedure for the presentation of Appropriation Bills.

(4) Where, in respect of a financial year, it is found that the amount of moneys appropriated by the Appropriation Act for any purpose to a government department is insufficient or that a need has arisen for expenditure for a purpose for which no sum of moneys has been appropriated by that Act, a supplementary estimate showing the sum of money required shall be laid before Parliament for its approval.

(5) Where in the case of a financial year, a supplementary estimate has been approved by Parliament in accordance with subsection (4), a supplementary Appropriation Bill shall be introduced into Parliament in the next financial year to provide for the appropriation of the sum approved for the purposes specified in that estimate.

(6) Notwithstanding the provisions of the preceding subsections of this section, the President may cause to be prepared and laid before Parliament, estimates of revenue and expenditure in the country for periods covering more than one year.

(7) This section shall not apply to a department or agency to which section 6 (2) (b) applies.

1.7. The Budget Cycle

A budget begins with agency requests sent to higher levels of the government administration. These requests often include justification and timelines for spending based on economic demographic forecast. The Government Agency's preparation and executive compilation may begin several months before the spending year begins.

The Budget cycle comprises a range of products and processes which feed into and flow from the Budget.

The Central Government budget cycle starts around May/June each year.

TEL: +233(0)548769918 /+233 (0) 501149296
Facebook Page: www.facebook.com/premiumicaglobal
Website: www.premiumonlinehub.com

Stages - Issue of Budget Circulars to all MDA's

1. Carrying out public expenditure survey.

Public Expenditure Survey It is a concept that has often preceded the preparation of Government budget. It is country wide approach of looking at the effect of past expenditures. It is normally carried out by a committee set up by the Minister of Finance. It is the annual review of public expenditure plans undertaken by Central Government and examining the impact of the various expenses on the nation. This originated from Committee Report in U.K. in 1961 that for efficient use of government resources, public expenditure survey should be carried out to assess the impact and benefit of the government expenditure (PESC). It is a survey carried out as a means to improve public expenditure control and benefit to the state.

2. Head of Budget development unit (BDU) of the MOFEP compiles reviews and updates the list of MDA beneficiaries.

3. Holding cross Sectoral meetings and policy hearings.

4. Determination of sectoral ceilings.

5. Workshop involving all MDAs to review GPRS, other medium term documents for the nation.

6. National Policy review workshop and intra sectoral meetings report submitted to the MOFEP.

7. MOFEP sets MDA ceilings and sends to Cabinet for review and approval.

8. After the approval of the ceilings, MOFEP shall issue Budget guidelines pertaining to the budget calendar.

9. Tax Revenue Estimates with the Revenue collecting Agencies.

10. MDA Budget Committee will submit MDA budget proposal for defence.

TEL: +233(0)548769918 /+233 (0) 501149296
Facebook Page: www.facebook.com/premiumicaglobal
Website: www.premiumonlinehub.com

11. After MDA defence MOFEP shall put together the entire national budget for Cabinet approval.

12. After cabinet review and final approval issue to MOFEP.

13. A date is fixed for the budget to be tabled before parliament by the Finance Minister.

14. After Finance Minister's presentation parliament will debate the budget.

15. After the debate, then Parliament will approve the budget.

1.8. Factors to be considered in government expenditure projections:

(i) Economic factors – for example inflation

(ii) What components of the government expenditure are susceptible to changes in which economic assumptions stated in (i) are applied.

(iii) Guidance from past expenditure patterns

(iv) Special expenditure in the budget year for example Electoral Commissions Budget in an election year.

> (v) What constraints on expenditure projections in revenue or financing.

1.9. Causes of failure to meet revenue targets

1. Corruption on the part of the staff of the revenue collecting Agencies.

2. Improper records keeping by the Tax Payers

3. Lack of motivation

TEL: +233(0)548769918 /+233 (0) 501149296
Facebook Page: www.facebook.com/premiumicaglobal
Website: www.premiumonlinehub.com

4. Revenue collection agencies not integrated

5. difficulty in locating Tax Payers in the informal sector

6. Lack of logistics for tax collection

7. Lack of training or revenue collecting officers.

2.0. Methods/ **Approaches to Budgeting (Types of Budgets Applied in the Public Sector):**

a. **Incremental Budgeting (IB)**

The term incremental budgeting is usually used to describe the traditional approach of setting a budget which is based on the current year's results plus an extra amount for estimated growth or anticipated rate of inflation in the coming year. It is recognized that it is an inefficient form of budgeting, because it encourages slack and wasteful spending also creeps into budgets. From budget preparation point of view it is fairly easy for Accountants or Administrators. This traditional approach to budgeting encourages work to be done on activity level and assessment of operational activities for the coming year. Because of the inefficiencies associated with incremental budgeting.

> **Features of Incremental Line Item Budgeting System**

i. The review of the current year's items against the budget which marks the beginning of the subsequent year's budget

ii. A distinction is made between committed and uncommitted items and resources

iii. A distinction is made between volume changes and price changes in localities

iv. A review is made of budgetary items which are deemed to be unachievable

TEL: +233(0)548769918 /+233 (0) 501149296
Facebook Page: www.facebook.com/premiumicaglobal
Website: www.premiumonlinehub.com

v. Consideration is made of financing changes in activities which are ceasing and current year's provision

vi. Provision is made for inflation

vii. Provision is made for contingencies and contributions to resources

viii. Provision is made for marginal changes between one year's and subsequent year's budget. Thus a current year's budget plus a percentage increase to attain the next year's budget.

    b. **Zero base budgeting** was therefore designed to get rid of this type of budgeting. This traditional incremental budgeting will be sufficient only if current operations are as effective, efficient and economical as they can be without any alternative courses of action available to the organization. The planning process should take account of alternative options and look for ways of improving performance.

In this approach, policy makers with a given situation (e.g. last year) as a base and make only marginal revision or adjustments for the current year. Management considers limited increases rather than focusing on major pragmatic concerns. Similarly the lecture focuses on individual expenditure rather than "the big picture". In this approach managers do not consider whether a particular item is still necessary. There is no prioritization. Once an item appears on the budget its inclusion in future budgets are taken for granted.

- **Advantages of ZBB**

i. It reveals items of expenditure within an organization which are not necessary are removed.
ii. It is possible to identify and remove inefficient or obsolete activities or operations.
iii. It adds a psychological impetus to employees to avoid wasteful spending

TEL: +233(0)548769918 /+233 (0) 501149296
Facebook Page: www.facebook.com/premiumicaglobal
Website: www.premiumonlinehub.com

iv. It brings in efficient allocation of resources to activities and departments.

c. Activity Based Budgeting:

This approach to budgeting is when the budget is prepared based on the specific activities or projects to be undertaken.

> ### Limitations of Activity Based Budgeting

i. It is prone to be over detailed.

ii. Too much details make the budget preparation cumbersome

iii. There is excessive centralized control over budget implementation

iv. ABB is fragmented

v. It is difficult to measure performance and output

vi. Absence of a real strategic focus in MDAs budget with limited linkages between resource allocation and policy objectives

d. Programme Based Budgeting (PBB):

Although the ABB has been used in Ghana since 1998 in the preparation of National Budget, it has its limitations as discussed above. And to overcome this limitation, the MoFEP introduced a more advanced and budgeting approach as the PBB.

Programme Based Budgeting is a budgeting approach which directly links the planned expenditures to clearly determined results and improved service delivery within the mandate of an organisation. The new approach simplifies the process of budget preparation and allows MDAs to be more strategic in their approach to budget management.
Performance indicators are also introduced to ensure performance measurement and assessment.

TEL: +233(0)548769918 /+233 (0) 501149296
Facebook Page: www.facebook.com/premiumicaglobal
Website: www.premiumonlinehub.com

> ➢ **Purposes of Programme Based Budgeting**

a. **Policy delivery:**
PBB specifically links resource allocations to MDA functions and its strategic policy objectives.

b. **Costing:**
PBB structures allow for the identification of necessary inputs to produce the core operations and projects required in order to contribute to strategic objectives.

c. **Performance:**
PBB provide a framework against which to measure the performance of MDA expenditure programme.

d. **Management Authority and Responsibility:**
PBB provides a management framework within which MDAs can effectively manage resources to achieve

> ➢ **Benefit of PBB**

- Ensure stronger linkage between public spending and determined results
- Ensure improved efficiency in the allocation and utilisation of resources
- Focus on more strategic budget information to promote understanding and debate in parliament
- Improve accuracy of budget information
- Shift emphasis of budget management from activities to delivery of outputs/results.

TEL: +233(0)548769918 /+233 (0) 501149296
Facebook Page: www.facebook.com/premiumicaglobal
Website: www.premiumonlinehub.com

> ➢ **Challenges faces by the PBB**

- Institutional arrangement
- Appointment of programme managers
- Capacity of MDAs
- Non- existence of dedicated budget staff
- Non- availability of baseline data
- Allocation of compensation of employees cost to programmes
- Weak monitoring and evaluation of mechanism

2.1. Budget revision may become necessary for the following reasons:-

(i) Significant changes in the National Budget as finally approved by Parliament.

(ii) Significant changes in the National wage Policy, Prices or Rates.

(iii) Unforeseen events particularly those that relate to project activity.

2.2. Circumstances for the request for supplementary estimate include: -

i. When the head of the department considers provided for existing activities for the financial year to be insufficient he/she shall prioritize the activities and ensure that only critical activities are carried out. However, if the prioritization will jeopardize the production of essential output the minister shall apply for supplementary estimate.

ii. Introduction of activities shall only be considered at a later date if its introduction will be of public interest. The minister of finance shall sign a certificate of urgency indicating the reasons for the introduction to Parliament.

TEL: +233(0)548769918 /+233 (0) 501149296
Facebook Page: www.facebook.com/premiumicaglobal
Website: www.premiumonlinehub.com

iii. Supplementary provision arising from general increase in cost of activities.

Application for supplementary estimate shall be included to the Minister of finance through the sector minister if the required additional fund is as a result of unforeseen increase in cost of activities.

iv. Application for supplementary activities shall be made if the introduction of a new activity is as a result of unforeseen natural occurrence.

2.3. Sources of financing deficit budget include

- Increase in taxation
- Removal of government subsidies
- Taking of external loans
- Taking of internal loans
- Printing of currency by the Bank of Ghana

2.4. Economic Implications

- Increase in taxation – this will erode the purchasing power of the people. The real income of the people will reduce and this can lead to recession.

- Removal of government subsidies - this can lead to inflation. Removal of subsidies shall make goods and services more expensive.

- Taking of external loans – this option is not viable as external borrowings are normally used for developmental projects.

- Taking of internal loans – it shall depend of the availability of disposable incomes.

TEL: +233(0)548769918 /+233 (0) 501149296
Facebook Page: www.facebook.com/premiumicaglobal
Website: www.premiumonlinehub.com

- Printing of currency by the Bank of Ghana – without a corresponding increase in goods and services, inflation can set in. printing of more currencies can lead to an increase in disposable income, higher demand for goods and services and ultimately increased economic activities and national income.

2.5. Sources of Government Domestic Borrowing

i. **Issue of securities**: - these are government borrowings through the issue of Treasury bills, Notes and Bonds on the domestic market.

ii. **Commercial Banks & Financial Institutions**:- these are long term loans borrowed from the domestic banking sector and non-banking sector like SSNIT.

iii. **Domestic Supplier Credit**: - these include the issue of letters of credit to local contractors to enable the contractors access credit facilities from banks. The contractors honour their obligations when the government pays them.

iv. **Advances from Bank of Ghana**: - these are monies advanced to the government by the Bank from their reserves. The advances are refunded when the government has sufficient revenue.

2.6. Central Investment Budgets

(i) COMMITMENT
It is the authorised commitment issue to public sector organization for them to incur on expenditure. It is recorded when purchase orders are issued or contract signed for goods and services. When the actual expenditure occurs, this only is reserved and the actual expenditure is recorded.

(ii**) FUND BALANCES** It means the net financial asset that is fund Financial Assets (ie cash, investment, receivables and other financial assets) less any fund related liabilities.

TEL: +233(0)548769918 /+233 (0) 501149296
Facebook Page: www.facebook.com/premiumicaglobal
Website: www.premiumonlinehub.com

(iii) **ALLOTMENT**: It is a periodic release of an appropriation. It helps keep departments from spending entire budget early in the fiscal year.

(iv) **PROVISIONAL WARRANT**

It is the authority issue by Minister of Finance for payments to be made in the first quarter of a year when budgets are not approved before the beginning of that year. It is based on Provisional Estimate.

(v) **REVOTE WARRANT**

When there is undischarged commitment the MOFEP prepares a revote schedule and issue a Revote Warrant to meet these undischarged commitments.

3.0. **Ghana Integrated Financial Management Information System (GIFMIS)**

Ghana Integrated Financial Management Information System (GIFMIS) is an integrated computerized financial management system for:

a.   Budget preparation;
b.   Budget Executive;
   -   Accounting and Financial Reporting
   -   Cash Management
c.   Assets management; and
d.   Human Resource and Payroll Management

3.1. **GIFMIS is one of the components of the Public Financial Management Reform Program (PUFMARP) which comprises the following**:

a.   Medium – Term Expenditure Framework (MTEF) (Budget preparation)
b.   Budget and Performance Monitoring Software (BPMS) now GIFMIS
c.   Integrated Personnel and Payroll Database (IPPD)
d.   Audit Reform (Internal Audit Agency, Act 2003)
e.   Procurement Reform (Public Procurement Act, 2003, Act 663)

TEL: +233(0)548769918 /+233 (0) 501149296
Facebook Page: www.facebook.com/premiumicaglobal
Website: www.premiumonlinehub.com

f. Legal and Regulatory Framework for Financial Reforms (FAA 2003 – Act 654 and FAR 2004- L.I. 1802)
g. Taxpayer Identification Numbering (e-Ghana Project)
h. Revenue Management (Ghana Revenue Authority Act 2009)
i. Aid and Debt Management System
j. Fiscal Decentralization (Local Government Finance Bill)

3.2. Objectives of GIFMIS

The primary aim is to establish an integrated ICA –based PFM Information System in Ghana at the MDAs located at National, Regional and District levels and MMDAs to improve efficiency in public financial management.

The secondary aims include:

a. Promote efficiency, transparency and accountability in public financial management through rationalisation and modernization of budgeting and public expenditure management of the Government of Ghana.
b. Promote timely dissemination of information for financial management
c. Rationalize the financial Administration Decree and Regulations.
d. Improve the efficiency and effectiveness of revenue collection of the Government of Ghana.
e. Maximize payment and commitment control

3.3. Specific PFM problems to be addressed by GIFMIS

a. Lack of interface/ integration between various PFM systems
b. Inadequate budgetary controls over public expenditure
c. Lack of transparency in budget execution
d. Poor record keeping on public financial transactions
e. Delay in financial reporting especially at the National level
f. Lack of uniform Charts of Accounts, which made the comparison performance of various budgets difficult.
g. Lack of timely, accurate and current information on budgetary allocations, commitments and actual revenue and expenditure.

3.4. GIFMIS Budget Modules

1. **Hyperion Planning plus:** for strategic planning aspect of the budget preparation process as well as analysis of the budget, e.g. Sensitivity and what if analysis.

2. **Hyperion Public Sector Planning and Budgeting:** for costing; thus the determination of the cost of items.

3. **Hyperion Project Financial Planning:** for project management including contract management.

3.5. GIFMIS modules

a. Procure-to-Pay (P2P)

P2P is an acronym of Oracle E-business suite application used for processing expenditure. It consists of Purchasing module, Accounts Payables module and Cash Management module.

- The **Purchasing** module is used for the preparation of Purchase Requisition, Purchase Order and Stores Receipts Advice.

- The **Accounts Payable module is used** for preparing Payment Vouchers, accounting for expenditure and tracking liabilities.

- **Cash Management** module is used for making Payments, Bank Reconciliation, cash forecasting

b. Oracle Hyperion

Oracle Hyperion is a GIFMIS application being used by the Government for preparation of the national budget. The key components and their functions are explained below:

TEL: +233(0)548769918 /+233 (0) 501149296
Facebook Page: www.facebook.com/premiumicaglobal
Website: www.premiumonlinehub.com

Hyperion Planning Plus – is used for the Strategic Planning aspect of the Budget preparation process as well as analysis of the budget, e.g. Sensitivity and what if analysis.

- **Hyperion Public Sector Planning and Budgeting** – is used for the Costing aspect of the budget process.

- **Hyperion Project Financial Planning** – is used for Project management including contract management

c. **Human Resource Management Information System (HRMIS)**

HRMIS is under the GIFMIS is being used by the government for human resource management. The aim is to automate public sector HR Management processes to improve efficiency and provide timely and accurate information for human resource management decisions in the public sector. The key components include:

- **Employee Profile Management -** for maintenance of the main bio data of employees from appointment to attrition in the areas of Employee Appointment, Employee record maintenance and Employee promotion.

- **Establishment Management** - for the management of Organizations, Locations, organizational hierarchies, Grades, Jobs, Positions and position hierarchies. This facilitates position control where no public institution (MDA/MMDA) on the HRMIS will exceed the established/approved staffing levels without approval from their appointing authorities.

- **Employee Cost Management -** for managing compensation of employees at all MDAs/MMDAs to ensure budgetary control over payroll cost

TEL: +233(0)548769918 /+233 (0) 501149296
Facebook Page: www.facebook.com/premiumicaglobal
Website: www.premiumonlinehub.com

d. **IPPD**

IPPD stands for integrated personnel payroll database. It is used for processing and payment of wages and salaries for public sector employees (workers at MDAs and MMDAs) at the Controller and Accountant General's Department. It is also use for processing and payment of pension allowances for some retired employees of government.

3.6. Key Users of GIFMIS

a. Budget officers
b. Accountants
c. Procurement officers
d. Store officers
e. Internal Auditors
f. Treasury officers
g. Administrators and HR Managers
h. Spending officers
i. Vote controllers
j. External Auditors

3.7. Benefit of GIFMIS

GIFMIS is important because of the following:

a. Improved budgetary, financial management (record keeping) and reporting processes
b. Provide accurate, timely and reliable financial information to Central Government and Decentralised Institutions and Organisations
c. Improvement in accountability, control monitoring and auditing of Government finances.
d. Enhance enforcement of financial legislation
e. Enhance and re-enforce the internal control systems in public management for accountability
f. Reduce manual processes, duplication of effort and errors.

Illustrative Format

TEL: +233(0)548769918 /+233 (0) 501149296
Facebook Page: www.facebook.com/premiumicaglobal
Website: www.premiumonlinehub.com

Statement of Comparison of Budget and Actual Amounts for Government XX for the Year ended December 31, 20XX

	Budgeted Amounts		Actual Amounts on Comparable Basis	Difference: Final Budget and Actual
	Original	Final		
RECEIPTS				
Taxation	XXX	XXX	XXX	XXX
International agencies	XXX	XXX	XXX	XXX
Other Grants and Aid	XXX	XXX	XXX	XXX
Proceeds: Disposal of Plant and Equipment	XXX	XXX	XXX	XXX
Trading activities	XXX	XXX	XXX	XXX
Other receipts	XXX	XXX	XXX	XXX
Total receipts	XXX	XXX	XXX	XXX
PAYMENTS				
Health	(XXX)	(XXX)	(XXX)	(XXX)
Education	(XXX)	(XXX)	(XXX)	(XXX)

TEL: +233(0)548769918 /+233 (0) 501149296
Facebook Page: www.facebook.com/premiumicaglobal
Website: www.premiumonlinehub.com

Public order	(XXX)	(XXX)	(XXX)	(XXX)
Social protection	(XXX)	(XXX)	(XXX)	(XXX)
Defence	(XXX)	(XXX)	(XXX)	(XXX)
Housing and Community amenities	(XXX)	(XXX)	(XXX)	(XXX)
Recreational cultural and religion	(XXX)	(XXX)	(XXX)	(XXX)
Economic affairs	(XXX)	(XXX)	(XXX)	(XXX)
Total payments	(XXX)	(XXX)	(XXX)	(XXX)
Net Receipts/ (Payments)	XXX	XXX	XXX	XXX

TEL: +233(0)548769918 /+233 (0) 501149296
Facebook Page: www.facebook.com/premiumicaglobal
Website: www.premiumonlinehub.com

FINANCIAL REPORTING IN THE PUBLIC SECTOR

OVERVIEW OF INTERNATIONAL PUBLIC SECTOR ACCOUNTING STANDARDS (IPSAS)

1.1. Introduction

International Public Sector Accounting Standards Board (IPSAB)

The International Public Sector Accounting Standards Board (IPSASB) which is a subsidiary body of the International Federation of Accountants (IFAC) develops accounting standards for public sector entities referred to as International Public Sector Accounting Standards (IPSASs).

The IPSASB's objective is to serve the public interest by developing high quality accounting standards and other publications for use by public sector entities around the world in the preparation of general purpose financial reports.

This is intended to enhance the quality and transparency of public sector financial reporting by providing better information for public sector financial management and decision making. In pursuit of this objective, the IPSASB supports the convergence of international and national public sector accounting standards and the convergence of accounting and statistical bases of financial reporting where appropriate; and also promotes the acceptance of its standards and other publications.

The adoption of IPSASs by governments will improve both **the quality** and **comparability** of financial information reported by public sector entities around the world. The IPSASB recognizes the right of governments and national standard-setters to establish accounting standards and guidelines for financial reporting in their jurisdictions. The IPSASB encourages the adoption of IPSASs and the harmonization of national requirements with IPSASs. Financial statements should be described as complying with IPSASs only if they comply with all the requirements of each applicable IPSAS.

TEL: +233(0)548769918 /+233 (0) 501149296
Facebook Page: www.facebook.com/premiumicaglobal
Website: www.premiumonlinehub.com

1.2. Objectives of the IPSASB

- To serve the public interest by developing high public sector financial reporting standards and other publications for use by public sector entities around the world in the preparation of general purpose financial reports.
- It facilitates the convergence of International and National standards
- Enhance the quality and uniformity of financial reporting through the world.

1.3. How IPSASB achieves its objectives

- The IPSASB achieves its objectives through the issuing of the IPSASs.
- It also issue Recommended Practice Guidelines (RPG) to provide guidance on good practice that public sector entities are encourage to follow.
- Promoting the acceptance and convergence of IPSASs to IFRSs.
- Publishing other documents which provide guidance on issues and experience in financial reporting in the public sector.

1.4. Scope of the Standards (IPSASs)

- The IPSASB develops IPSASs which apply to both accrual and cash basis of accounting.
- The IPSASs set out **recognition, measurement, presentation and disclosure requirement** dealing with transactions and events in general purpose financial statements.
- The IPSASs are designed to apply to the general purpose financial statements of all public sector entities.
- Any limitation of the applicability of specific IPSAS is made clear in those standards.
- The IPSASB has adopted the policy that all paragraphs in IPSASs have equal authority.

TEL: +233(0)548769918 /+233 (0) 501149296
Facebook Page: www.facebook.com/premiumicaglobal
Website: www.premiumonlinehub.com

1.5. Benefits of Transition to Accrual Accounting

- There is adequate matching and accruals of revenue and expenditure (including depreciation)
- It is easy to compare the performance and financial statements of the Public sector entities with private sector entities.
- The Net Book Value of assets can easily be determined in the balance sheet.
- It provides the Government with update of the fiscal position of the state by bringing all assets and liabilities into the balance sheet.

1.6. Reasons for Adoption of IPSAS

The driving forces for the adoption of the IPSASs by Governments across the globe can be summarized as follows:

- **International Trends**: There are a lot of countries around the world which have already adopted and implemented the IPSASs in the preparation and presentation of general purpose financial statements. And as such, it has become a trend that to be able to effective show the financial performance and position of the Government for the year, the usage of the IPSASs will be best and adequate.

- **Pressure from Donor Community**: Due to the continuous Budget Deficit of mostly developing countries, there is always a need to obtain grants from other developed countries, International Bodies, among others. As such, these donors require a proper preparation of the financial statement of the Government through the adoption and implementation of the IPSASs.

- **Enhancement of Government Financial Reporting**: Since the IPSASs are similar to the IFRSs used by the private sector entities in the preparation and presentation of financial statements, the adoption and implementation of the IPSASs by Government will improve the Financial Reporting.

TEL: +233(0)548769918 /+233 (0) 501149296
Facebook Page: www.facebook.com/premiumicaglobal
Website: www.premiumonlinehub.com

- **International Harmonization:** Since major developed countries such as the United States of America (USA) among others have already adopted and implemented the IPSASs in the preparation and presentation of Financial statements by the Government (s), it has become a norm to encourage other Governments to also implement the standards to enhance the comparability of the financial statements of Government across the globe as being done already in the private sector.

- **There is Better Financial Information Supports.**

1.7. Pre – Conditions for Implementation of Accrual Accounting

There are a number of prerequisite to the successful implementation of accounting reforms in a Government organization. These are:

- Consultation and Acceptance among Public Department/Government departments and Agencies.
- Participation of the Accounting Profession: It is important for the effective and efficient management of the public service for the Institute of Chartered Accountants – Ghana to participate and contribute towards the adoption and implementation of the IPSASs.
- There has to be support of Government Auditor. Thus the Auditor General as well as the Controller and Accountant General.
- Comprehensive Management Training: To effectively and efficiently operate the IPSASs, departmental managers must be trained to use an accrual accounting system and to achieve the benefits from its operation. This is important because, they are used to the Cash basis accounting system.
- A recognition of elapsed time is needed
- The application of User – Friendly computer Technology
- Economy: The benefits of the adoption and implementation of IPSASs should not outweigh the cost.
- Budgetary and Accounting Code Structure: The adoption may require the adoption of new chart of accounts.

TEL: +233(0)548769918 /+233 (0) 501149296
Facebook Page: www.facebook.com/premiumicaglobal
Website: www.premiumonlinehub.com

- Phased Implementation: The implementation must be sequential. It can first start in the Central Accounts Department and then for a number of years be implemented in other MDAs and MMDAs.

1.8. Measures Involved In The Implementation of Accrual Based Accounting

- Modification of existing laws and rules to introduce the double – entry accounting system.
- Appointments of consultants for the development of state manual
- Completion and adoption of the manual
- Personnel training
- Valuation of assets and liabilities
- Production or preparation of financial statements
- The Audit of financial statements.

1.9. Problems on Adoption of IPSASs

- **The degree of Entrenchment of existing system**: The adoption of the IPSASs is against the laws and rules which has been made known to the government officials from the 1992 Constitution of Ghana. As such, it makes most government reluctant to the adoption.

- **Cost of Implementation:** From the measures involved in the implementation of the IPSASs discussed above, it can be concluded that the adoption is a capital investment which requires a lot of finance. However, since most developing countries are already struggling with their already existing budget for National development, the adoption may not be appropriate.

- **Availability of Qualified Accountants**: In most developing countries, the Government may be incapable of employing and paying Qualified Chartered Accounts to work in the various public sector entities. However, the private sector entities are ready to pay for the service of these qualifies accountants. This has led to

TEL: +233(0)548769918 /+233 (0) 501149296
Facebook Page: www.facebook.com/premiumicaglobal
Website: www.premiumonlinehub.com

the unavailability of professional accountants in the public sector and enhance difficult in the application of the IPSASs when adopted.

- Readiness of Government Departments and Agencies.

- Resistance from the MDAs and MMDAs.

2. **FINANCIAL STATEMENTS IN THE PUBLIC SECTOR**
   a. Statement of Financial Performance
   b. Statement of Financial Position
   c. Statement of Cash flow

3. **The International Public Sector Accounting Standards (IPSASs)**

The IPSASs are as follows

IPSAS 1 - Presentation of Financial Statements
IPSAS 2 - Cash Flow Statements
IPSAS 3 - Accounting Policies, Changes in Accounting Estimates and Errors
IPSAS 4 - The Effects of Changes in Foreign Exchange Rates
IPSAS 5 - Borrowing Costs
IPSAS 6 - Consolidated and Separate Financial Statements
IPSAS 7 - Investments in Associates
IPSAS 8 - Interests in Joint Ventures
IPSAS 9 - Revenue from Exchange Transactions
IPSAS 10 - Financial Reporting in Hyperinflationary Economies
IPSAS 11 - Construction Contracts
IPSAS 12 - Inventories
IPSAS 13 – Leases

IPSAS 14 - Events after the Reporting Date

IPSAS 15 - Financial Instruments: Disclosure and Presentation
IPSAS 16 - Investment Property
IPSAS 17 - Property, Plant, and Equipment
IPSAS 18 - Segment Reporting

TEL: +233(0)548769918 /+233 (0) 501149296
Facebook Page: www.facebook.com/premiumicaglobal
Website: www.premiumonlinehub.com

IPSAS 19 - Provisions, Contingent Liabilities and Contingent Assets

IPSAS 20 - Related Party Disclosures

IPSAS 21 - Impairment of Non-Cash-Generating Assets

IPSAS 22 - Disclosure of Financial Information about the General Government Sector

IPSAS 23 - Revenue from Non-Exchange Transactions (Taxes and Transfers)

IPSAS 24 - Presentation of Budget Information in Financial Statements

IPSAS 25 - Employee Benefits

NOTE: It must be noted that, these IPSASs have almost the same effects as what is known in Financial Accounting, Financial Reporting and Corporate Reporting (thus Private sector accounting) as the International Accounting Standards(IASs) and International Financial Reporting Standards (IFRSs).

3.1. IPSAS 1 - Presentation of Financial Statements

Scope:

This standard applies to the presentation of all general purpose financial statements prepared and presented under the accrual basis of accounting in accordance with the IPSASs.

3.1.1. Objectives of General Purpose Financial Statements (GPFS)

To provide information used for decision – making, and to demonstrate the accountability of the public entities for the resources entrusted to it by:

- Providing information about the sources, allocation and uses of financial resources.
- Providing information about how the entities financed its activities and met its requirement.
- Providing information about how the evaluating of the entity's ability to finance its activities and meet its liabilities and commitment.

TEL: +233(0)548769918 /+233 (0) 501149296
Facebook Page: www.facebook.com/premiumicaglobal
Website: www.premiumonlinehub.com

- Providing information about the financial conditions of the entity and changes in it.
- Providing information for the evaluation of the overall performance of an entity.

3.1.2. Components of Financial Statements

- Statement of Financial Performance (Statement of Profit or Loss)
- Statement of Financial Position (Balance Sheet)
- Statement of Changes in Equity
- Cash flow statement
- Statement of Comparison of Budget and Actual Amounts
- Accounting Policies and Notes to Financial Statements.

Note: You can refer to IAS 1 – Presentation of Financial Statements

3.1.3. Qualitative Characteristics of Financial Statements

These are the set of attributes that make the information in the financial statement useful to users. The four principal qualitative characteristics are

Presentation	Content
Understandability	Relevance
Comparability	Reliability

The Framework considers the **materiality** of a transaction as a threshold (cut-off point) quality. Financial information is said to be material if its omission or misstatement can influence the economic decisions of users taken on the basis of the financial statements. Therefore all the four qualitative characteristics above are subject to materiality. This means

TEL: +233(0)548769918 /+233 (0) 501149296
Facebook Page: www.facebook.com/premiumicaglobal
Website: www.premiumonlinehub.com

that any information that is not material may not be relevant or reliable and may not affect understandability or comparability.

a. RELEVANCE

Financial information is relevant if it has the ability to influence the economic decisions of users. It must have predictive or confirmatory value. Predictive value assists users to evaluate past, present or future events. Confirmatory value helps users to confirm or correct past evaluations. Note that by highlighting unusual transactions in the accounts predictability is enhanced.

Relevance of information is affected by

its nature	materiality
Nature alone may be sufficient to determine relevance.	Information is material if its omission or misstatement could influence the economic decisions of users taken on the basis of the financial statements.
	Depends on size of item or error judged in the particular circumstances of its omission or misstatement
	a threshold or cut-off point rather than being a primary qualitative

	characteristic.

b. RELIABILITY

Reliable information is one that is free from material error and bias. The following qualities make information reliable:

a) **Faithful representation**: information must represent faithfully the effects of transactions and other events that it purports to represent. This is only possible if a transaction is accounted for according to its economic substance and not its mere legal form. For example, this is why internally generated goodwill is not recognised in the accounts. It is also applied in lease agreements.

b) **Completeness**: Financial information will be reliable if it is complete, subject to the constraint of materiality and cost.

c) **Neutrality:** This means that any judgments exercised in the preparation of financial statements must be free from bias. That is, the judgment exercise should not influence the user to make a decision in order to achieve a predetermined outcome. Neutrality is needed in areas such as valuation of inventory, provisions, etc.

d) **Prudence:** This demands the exercise of caution in estimating the outcome of uncertain events. This forbids the accountant to anticipate profit but requires him to make provision for all foreseeable losses.

c. COMPARABILITY

Financial statements should be comparable with the financial statements of other companies and with the financial statements of the same company for earlier periods. This is achieved through consistency of treatments and disclosure of accounting policies.

d. UNDERSTANDABILITY

TEL: +233(0)548769918 /+233 (0) 501149296
Facebook Page: www.facebook.com/premiumicaglobal
Website: www.premiumonlinehub.com

Users must be able to understand financial statements. Therefore, in preparing the financial statements, a reasonable knowledge of business and accounting by users is assumed. Understandability depends on users' ability as well as the aggregation and classification made.

3.1.3.   Balance Between the Qualitative Characteristics

Some of the characteristics discussed above are conflicting. For example, information that is complete may not be understandable as a result of too much detail. Also information that is prudent may not be neutral as a result of the subjectivity involved in estimating the outcome of uncertain transactions. Furthermore, information that is relevant must be timely so that it is not out-of-date. However, the reliability characteristics may be affected if time is not allowed for all uncertainties to be resolved.

Note that in striking a balance between the qualitative characteristics, the overriding consideration is how best to satisfy the economic decision-making needs of users.
Finally the benefit to be derived from the financial information should exceed the cost of providing it.

3.1.4.   Definitions

An asset is

- a resource controlled by the enterprise
- as a result of past events
- from which future economic benefits are expected to flow.

A liability is
- a present obligation of the enterprise
- arising from past events
- settlement of which is expected to result in an outflow of resources embodying economic benefits.

Equity

TEL: +233(0)548769918 /+233 (0) 501149296
Facebook Page: www.facebook.com/premiumicaglobal
Website: www.premiumonlinehub.com

- the residual interest
- in the assets of the enterprise
- after deducting all its liabilities.

Income
- increases in economic benefits during the accounting period
- in the form of inflows (or enhancements) of assets or decreases of liabilities
- that result in increases in equity
- other than those relating to contributions from equity participants.

Expenses
- decreases in economic benefits during the accounting period
- in the form of outflows (or depletions) of assets or incurrences of liabilities
- that result in decreases in equity
- other than those relating to distributions to equity participants

3.1.5. Recognition of the Elements of Financial Statements

Certain items may meet the definition of the elements but may still not be recognised in financial statements because they must also meet certain recognition criteria.

The framework explains recognition as "the process of incorporating in the statement of financial position or statement of comprehensive income an item that meets the definition of an element and satisfies the following criteria for recognition:

a. it is probable that any future economic benefits associated with the item will flow to or from the entity; and
b. the item has a value that can be measured with reliability.

TEL: +233(0)548769918 /+233 (0) 501149296
Facebook Page: www.facebook.com/premiumicaglobal
Website: www.premiumonlinehub.com

PUBLIC SECTOR ENTITY – STATEMENT OF FINANCIAL PERFORMANCE FOR THE YEAR ENDED DECEMBER 31 20X2

REVENUE:	20X2	20X1
Taxes	Xxx	Xxx
Fees, fines, penalties & licence	Xxx	Xxx
Revenue from exchange transfers	Xxx	Xxx
Transfer from other government entities	Xxx	Xxx
Other revenue	Xxx	Xxx
Total revenue(a)	Xxx	Xxx

EXPENSES:		
Wages, salaries & emoluments	Xxx	xxx
Grants and other transfer payments	Xxx	Xxx
Supplies and consumables used	Xxx	Xxx
Depreciation and amortisation	Xxx	xxx
Impairment of PPE	Xxx	Xxx

TEL: +233(0)548769918 /+233 (0) 501149296
Facebook Page: www.facebook.com/premiumicaglobal
Website: www.premiumonlinehub.com

Other expenses	Xxx	Xxx
Finance cost	Xxx	Xxx
Total expenses (b)	Xxx	Xxx
Surplus /(deficit)(a –b)	Xxx	xxx

STATEMENT OF FINANCIAL POSITION

	20X2	20X1
ASSETS:		
Current assets:		
Cash and cash equivalent	Xxx	Xxx
Receivables	Xxx	Xxx
Inventories	Xxx	Xxx
Prepayment of expenses	Xxx	xxx
Short term investments	Xxx	Xxx
	xxx	Xxx
Non- current assets:		
Long term investment	Xxx	Xxx

TEL: +233(0)548769918 /+233 (0) 501149296
Facebook Page: www.facebook.com/premiumicaglobal
Website: www.premiumonlinehub.com

Infrastructure, Plant & Equipment	Xxx	Xxx
Receivables	Xxx	Xxx
Other financial assets	Xxx	Xxx
Land and Building	Xxx	Xxx
Intangible assets	Xxx	Xxx
Other non- financial assets	Xxx	Xxx
	xxx	Xxx
Total assets (a)	Xxx	Xxx

Liabilities:

Current liabilities:

Payables	Xxx	Xxx
Short term borrowing	Xxx	Xxx
Provisions	Xxx	Xxx
Employees benefits	Xxx	xxx
Superannuation/retirement payment	Xxx	Xxx

TEL: +233(0)548769918 /+233 (0) 501149296
Facebook Page: www.facebook.com/premiumicaglobal
Website: www.premiumonlinehub.com

	Xxx	xxx
Non – current liabilities		
Long term loan	Xxx	Xxx
Others	Xxx	Xxx
	Xxx	xxx
Total liability (b)	Xxx	xxx
Net assets (a – b)	Xxx	Xxx
Equity:		
Capital contributed by other government entities	Xxx	xxx
Reserves	Xxx	xxx
Accumulated surplus/ (deficit)	Xxx	Xxx
Total Equity/ Net assets	xxx	xxx

TEL: +233(0)548769918 /+233 (0) 501149296
Facebook Page: www.facebook.com/premiumicaglobal
Website: www.premiumonlinehub.com

WORKINGS

a. **Direct Tax**	$m	b. **Indirect Tax**	$m
Tax paid by individuals	Xxx	General taxes on Goods and services	Xxx
Tax paid by corporates	Xxx	Excise	Xxx
Miscellaneous taxes	Xxx	Customs and other input duties	Xxx
Receivables (Note)	Xxx	Taxes on export	Xxx
	Xxx	Levies	Xxx
		Receivables (Notes)	Xxx
			Xxx
c. **Non – Tax Revenue**	$m	d. **Compensation for Employees**	$m
Property Income	Xxx	Established post	Xxx
Revenue from sale of Goods or services	Xxx	Non – established post	Xxx
Fines, penalties and forfeiture	Xxx	Gratuities	Xxx
Miscellaneous Tax Revenue	Xxx	Casual labour	Xxx
	Xxx	End of service benefits	Xxx
		Salary arrears (Notes)	Xxx
			Xxx

TEL: +233(0)548769918 /+233 (0) 501149296
Facebook Page: www.facebook.com/premiumicaglobal
Website: www.premiumonlinehub.com

e. **Goods and Services**	$m	f. Public debt	$m
Repairs and maintenance	Xxx	Domestic debt interest	Xxx
Administration cost	Xxx	External debt interest	Xxx
Consultancy expenses	Xxx	Interest outstanding (Notes)	Xxx
Conferences and services	Xxx		xxx
Special services cost	Xxx		
External travels	Xxx	g. **Subsidies**	$m
Internal travel	Xxx	Utilities	Xxx
Rentals	Xxx	Consumption	Xxx
Outstanding (Notes)	<u>Xxx</u>	Petroleum products	Xxx
	<u>Xxx</u>	Production	<u>Xxx</u>
			<u>Xxx</u>
h. **Grants**	$m		
Grant paid	Xxx		
DACF arrears	Xxx		
Other grants	<u>Xxx</u>		
	<u>Xxx</u>		

TEL: +233(0)548769918 /+233 (0) 501149296
Facebook Page: www.facebook.com/premiumicaglobal
Website: www.premiumonlinehub.com

i. Non – Financial Assets	$m	j. Domestic Debt	$m
Motor vehicle	Xxx	Treasury bills	Xxx
Equipment	Xxx	Bonds	Xxx
Aircraft	Xxx	Other domestic debts/loans	Xxx
Infrastructure	Xxx		Xxx
	Xxx		
Consumption of fixed capital	Xxx		
Net Book Value	xxx		
k. External Debt	$m	l. Accumulated Fund	$m
Bilateral and Multilateral	Xxx	Balance c/f	Xxx
Euro Bonds	Xxx	Surplus/(deficits)	Xxx
Loans from other external entities	Xxx		xxx
	xxx		
m. Payables	$m		
Salaries (working)	Xxx		

TEL: +233(0)548769918 /+233 (0) 501149296
Facebook Page: www.facebook.com/premiumicaglobal
Website: www.premiumonlinehub.com

Goods and Services (working)	Xxx
Interest (working)	Xxx
DACF (working)	Xxx
	Xxx

TEL: +233(0)548769918 /+233 (0) 501149296
Facebook Page: www.facebook.com/premiumicaglobal
Website: www.premiumonlinehub.com

3.2. **IPSAS 2 : CASH FLOW STATEMENT**

SCOPE:

An entity that prepares and presents financial statements under the accrual basis of accounting shall prepare a Cash Flow statement in accordance with the requirement of this standard.

3.2.1. Usefulness of the Cash Flow Statement
- To enable the assessment of the entity's cash flows
- To enable the assessment of the entity's compliance with legislation and regulations.
- To enable stakeholders in making decision about whether to provide resources to, or enter into transaction with the entity.

3.2.2. **Presenting of Cash flow statement**

As you already know in IAS 7 Presentation of the Cash flow statement, the statement is presented with three sub headings known as activities. These includes; **Operating activities, Investing activities and Financing activities.**

TEL: +233(0)548769918 /+233 (0) 501149296
Facebook Page: www.facebook.com/premiumicaglobal
Website: www.premiumonlinehub.com

FORMAT:

Public Sector Entity – Cash Flow statement for the year ended December 31 20x2

Cash flow from operating activities	20X1	20X2
Receipt:		
Taxation	Xxx	Xxx
Sales of goods and services	Xxx	Xxx
Interest received	Xxx	Xxx
Other receipts	Xxx	Xxx
Payment:		
Employee costs	(Xxx)	(Xxx)
Superannuation	(Xxx)	(Xxx)
Supplier	(Xxx)	(Xxx)
Interest paid	(Xxx)	(Xxx)
Other payments	(Xxx)	(Xxx)
Net cash flows from operating activities (a)	(Xxx)/xxx	(xxx)/xxx

Cash flows from investing

TEL: +233(0)548769918 /+233 (0) 501149296
Facebook Page: www.facebook.com/premiumicaglobal
Website: www.premiumonlinehub.com

activities:

Purchases of Fixed assets	(Xxx)	(xxx)
Proceeds from the sale of fixed asset	Xxx	Xxx
Proceeds from the sale of investment properties	Xxx	Xxx
Purchase of foreign currency securities	(xxx)	(xxx)
Other investment	Xxx/(xxx)	Xxx/(xxx)
Net cash flow from investing activities (b)	Xxx/(xxx)	Xxx/(xxx)

Cash flow from Financing activities:

Proceeds from borrowing	Xxx	Xxx
Payment of borrowing	(xxx)	(xxx)
Dividend payment	(xxx)	(xxx)
Net cash flow from financing activities (c)	Xxx/(xxx)	Xxx/(xxx)
Net increase/(decrease) in cash and cash equivalents (a + b+ c)	Xxx/(xxx)	Xxx/(xxx)

TEL: +233(0)548769918 /+233 (0) 501149296
Facebook Page: www.facebook.com/premiumicaglobal
Website: www.premiumonlinehub.com

Cash and cash equivalent at the beginning of the period	Xxx/(xxx)	Xxx/(xxx)
Cash and cash equivalent at the end of the period	Xxx/(xxx)	Xxx/(xxx)

NOTES TO THE CASH FLOW   **STATEMENT**

(a) **Cash and cash equivalent**	20X1	20X2
Cash on hand and balance with bank	Xxx	Xxx
Short term investment	Xxx	Xxx
	xxx	Xxx

(b) **Reconciliation of Net**	**Cash Flows from operating**	**Activities to surplus/ (deficit)**
	20X1	20X2
Surplus/ (deficit)	Xxx/(xxx)	Xxx/(xxx)

Non cash movement:

TEL: +233(0)548769918 /+233 (0) 501149296
Facebook Page: www.facebook.com/premiumicaglobal
Website: www.premiumonlinehub.com

Depreciation	Xxx	Xxx
Amortisation	Xxx	Xxx
Increase in provision for doubtful debt	Xxx	Xxx
Increase in payables	Xxx	xxx
Increase in borrowing	Xxx	Xxx
Increase in provision for employment cost	Xxx	xxx
Loss on the sale of PPE	Xxx	Xxx
Profit on the sale of PPE	(xxx)	(xxx)
Increase in current assets	(xxx)	(xxx)
Decrease in current assets	Xxx	Xxx
Net cash flow from operating	Xxx	xxx

3.3. IPSAS 3: Accounting Policies, Changes In Accounting Estimates and Errors

Note that this has almost the same application as **IAS 8**

If the company is going to use another accounting policy this year and find an error relating to last year's account then the company should adjust for this year and last year's financial statements.(Retrospective adjusting)

TEL: +233(0)548769918 /+233 (0) 501149296
Facebook Page: www.facebook.com/premiumicaglobal
Website: www.premiumonlinehub.com

If the company is going to use another accounting estimate this year and the company should adjust for current year financial statements and future one. (Prospective adjusting)

But how to determine whether this is a change in accounting policy or estimate?
Well, if there's a change in

- **Measurement basis** of the figure, e.g., value the inventory using FIFO but now use weighted average method; use replacement cost rather than historic cost.

- **Recognition basis** of the figure, e.g., recognize as an expense before but now for asset (e.g., AS 23 borrowing costs)

- **Presentation basis** of the figure, e.g., recognize the depreciation expense into cost of sales now rather than in administrative expenses before.

You are going to change in the accounting policy only if:
1. a change in laws / accounting standards and you are required to do so;
2. gives a fairer presentation to the users of FS.

And anything that is not changing the measurement, recognition or presentation of figures are deemed to be a change in accounting estimate such as:
- Allowance for receivables;
- Useful life/ depreciation method of the non-current assets;
- Warranty provision relating to return of goods from customers.

An error may happen if there's a

- Misuse of the accounting standard last year;

TEL: +233(0)548769918 /+233 (0) 501149296
Facebook Page: www.facebook.com/premiumicaglobal
Website: www.premiumonlinehub.com

- Fraud happened last year;
- Omit some figures in last year's account.

4. **Changes in accounting policy this year:**

Assume it happens in last year as well and of course this year happens;
Adjust for last year closing retained earnings taken into account in the changes to be brought forward in this year's statement of changes in equity.

5. **Material prior period errors found:**

Correct last year's material errors;
Adjust for last year closing retained earnings taken into account in the error effect to be brought forward in this year's statement of changes in equity.

6. **Changes in accounting estimate:**
Use the new one to continue the calculation.

3.4. **IPSAS 14: Events After The reporting period / date**

Note that this has almost the same effect as **IAS 10.**

This is the event happened between financial statement year end and the financial statements are authorized to be issued to the shareholders to be discussed at the AGM (annual general meeting).

They will be either **adjusting** events or **non-adjusting** events

Magical way to distinguish the adjusting events and non-adjusting events:

TEL: +233(0)548769918 /+233 (0) 501149296
Facebook Page: www.facebook.com/premiumicaglobal
Website: www.premiumonlinehub.com

Is it because of this event then it will affect the figure as at the year end?

- **Adjusting events**

- Change in judgments, estimate or assumptions after the year end.
e.g., 1, inventory sold at a loss? Change in assumptions that closing inventory should be valued at the lower of cost and net realizable value (IAS 2); 2, Customers go bankruptcy so that recoverability of the receivable balance at the year-end has been changed.
3, If company is involved in going concern problems after the year end and because the financial statement should be prepared under going concern basis and now this is changed.

- The settlement after the reporting date of a court case that confirms that the entity had a present obligation at the end of the reporting date.
- Indications of the impairments of assets at the reporting date.
- The amount of revenue for sharing between government departments
- The determination of bonus payments if the entity had a present legal or constructive obligation at the reporting date.
- The discovery of fraud or errors that shows that the financial statements were incorrect.

- **Non-adjusting events**

There's no link between financial statement figures at the year end and events after the FS year end.
e.g., 1, fire destroyed the inventory after the year end (can't predict!)
2, dividends are declared after the year end or share issues after the year end (no link between figures and events)

- Change in revaluation policy

TEL: +233(0)548769918 /+233 (0) 501149296
Facebook Page: www.facebook.com/premiumicaglobal
Website: www.premiumonlinehub.com

NOTE: Students are encouraged to read through the rest of the Standards not purposely for the examination but also for effective and efficient application later in practice.

TEL: +233(0)548769918 /+233 (0) 501149296
Facebook Page: www.facebook.com/premiumicaglobal
Website: www.premiumonlinehub.com

ACCOUNTING FOR PUBLIC PRIVATE PARTNERSHIPS (PPPs)

According to Government of Ghana National Policy on Public Private Partnership, "Public Private Partnership is a contractual arrangement between a public entity and a private sector party, with clear agreement on shared objectives for the provision of public infrastructure and services traditionally provided by the public sector".

The World Bank Public Private Partnerships Reference Guide, 2012 also defined Public Private Partnership as "a long –term contract between a private party and a government agency, for providing a public assets or service, in which the private party bears significant risk and management responsibility".

Usually, in a PPP arrangement the private sector party performs part or all of a government's service delivery functions, and assumes the associated risk for a significant period of time. In return, the private sector party receives a benefit or financial remuneration (according to predefined performance criteria), which may be derived:

- *Entirely from service tariffs or user charges;*
- *Entirely from Government budgets, which may be fixed or partially fixed, periodic payments (annuities) and contingent; or*
- *A combination of the above*

3. **Objectives of the PPPs**

The key objectives of this policy are to:

e. *Leverage public assets and funds with private sector resources from local and international markets to accelerate needed investments in infrastructure and services*

TEL: +233(0)548769918 /+233 (0) 501149296
Facebook Page: www.facebook.com/premiumicaglobal
Website: www.premiumonlinehub.com

    f.   *Encourage and facilitate investment by the private sector by creating as enabling environment for PPPs where value for money for government can be clearly demonstrated.*

    g.   *Increase the availability of public infrastructure and services and improve service quality and efficiency of projects;*

    h.   *Protect the interest of all stakeholders including end users, affected people, government and the private sector.*

    i.   *Ensure attainment of required and acceptable local and international social and environmental standards*

    j.   *Provide a framework for developing efficient risk sharing mechanisms.*

The benefits of PPPs include the following:

a) Accelerated delivery of needed infrastructure and public services on time and within budget.

b) Encouraging the private sector to provide innovative design, technology and financing structures.

c) Increased international and domestic investment.

d) Risk sharing by government with private sector partners.

e) Ensuring good quality public services and their wider availability.

f) Real financial benefits reflected in reduction in the initial public capital outlay, and a better utilization and allocation of public funds.

g) Economic growth and increased and wider employment possibilities.

h) Technology transfer and capacity building

i) Improved operation and maintenance of public infrastructure

TEL: +233(0)548769918 /+233 (0) 501149296
Facebook Page: www.facebook.com/premiumicaglobal
Website: www.premiumonlinehub.com

Guiding Principles for PPPs

All PPP arrangements in Ghana shall be guided by the following principles:

a. **Value for money**: Value for money is paramount and PPPs should give greater value for money than the best realistic public sector project designed to achieve similar service outputs. Achieving value for money is a key requirement of government at all stages of a project's development and procurement and is a combination of the service outcome to be delivered by the private sector, together with the degree of risk transfer and financial implications for government. Value for money is the driver for adopting the PPP approach, rather than capital scarcity or the balance sheet treatment.

b. **Risk allocation**: An efficient risk allocation is vital in determining whether value for money can be achieved in PPP projects. GoG's principle with regards to risk allocation shall be used to optimise, rather than maximise, the transfer of project risks to the private party. Risks will therefore be allocated to the party best able to control and manage them in such a manner that value for money is maximised. The allocation of risk will therefore determine the chosen method of private sector involvement and allocation of responsibilities, which shall take into account the protection of the public interest.

c. **Ability to pay**: End user ability to pay shall be a key consideration for all PPP projects. The PPP option must demonstrate long-term affordability to the public and overall Government budgetary sustainability, forward commitments in relation to public expenditure and the potential for returns on private sector investment, given other priorities and commitments.

d. **Local content & technology transfer**: PPP projects shall be structured to encourage the maximum use of local content and technology transfer. As much as possible, the PPP arrangement

TEL: +233(0)548769918 /+233 (0) 501149296
Facebook Page: www.facebook.com/premiumicaglobal
Website: www.premiumonlinehub.com

shall facilitate the promotion of local industries and the private sector in Ghana.

e. **Safeguarding Public Interest and Consumer Rights**: GoG is committed to ensuring that each PPP project shall have positive impact upon the public interest. The following principles shall be addressed in PPP transactions:

- Safeguards to users particularly vulnerable groups;

- Setting affordable user charges and tariff structures

f. **Environmental, Climate and Social Safeguards:** The Government shall ensure that PPP activities conform to the environmental laws of Ghana and the highest standards of environmental, climate and social safeguards.

Furthermore, all PPP projects shall be governed in accordance with the following:

i. **Clear objectives and output requirements:** PPP projects shall take into account the expected outputs of each project, allowing for optimal risk transfer to the private party and thereby ensure greater value for money for the public sector.

ii. **Accountability:** As a means of good governance PPP projects must ensure accountability:

- Every stage of the PPP arrangement shall follow laid-down procedures and regulations.

- Decisions must be objective and in consonance with law and government policies.
- Public sector entities undertaking PPPs must follow prescribed processes for decision-making within their organizations.

TEL: +233(0)548769918 /+233 (0) 501149296
Facebook Page: www.facebook.com/premiumicaglobal
Website: www.premiumonlinehub.com

iii. **Transparency**: Principles of transparency shall guide all PPP projects:

– There must be a well-defined procurement process for the PPP. Instructions to bidders must be clear and unambiguous to prevent manipulation or abuse of the process. The bid conditions and evaluation criteria must lead to the attainment of value for money, economy, and efficiency and must be made available to all interested private sector parties.

– Where a decision is taken to consider an unsolicited bid, there must be clear and objective reasons supporting the decision which shall be in conformity with this policy.

– The process shall be accessible to the public to the extent allowed by law except where national security would be prejudiced.

– Equal opportunity and access to information must be given to all interested bidders.

iv. **Competition**: As much as feasible all PPP projects should be subjected to a competitive process so as to obtain value for money and efficiency.

v. **Contracting Authority, ownership and commitment**: Contracting Authorities shall have the primary responsibility for managing the process and implementing the project.

vi. **Stakeholder Consultation Process**: Contracting authorities shall ensure adequate stakeholder consultation, understanding and support in advance of entering into a PPP arrangement and shall endeavour to identify relevant stakeholders and undertake comprehensive consultation and awareness of PPP projects under consideration.

TEL: +233(0)548769918 /+233 (0) 501149296
Facebook Page: www.facebook.com/premiumicaglobal
Website: www.premiumonlinehub.com

BIBLIOGRAPHY:

- ❖ Institute of Chartered Accountants – Ghana Study Text – Public Sector Accounting
- ❖ Author's Library
- ❖ Premium Education Hub's Library and Research Department
- ❖ Google.com
- ❖ Wikipedia.com
- ❖ Among other websites and books that were used.

TEL: +233(0)548769918 /+233 (0) 501149296
Facebook Page: www.facebook.com/premiumicaglobal
Website: www.premiumonlinehub.com